Youth, Education and Work in Europe

The transition from school to work is a crucial problem for young people today in both East and West European countries. In this time of economic crisis, many young people face unemployment or under-employment, the lack of economic security, and the exclusion from active, socially responsible or rewarding professional and civic roles both within and outside the workplace.

This collection of essays deals with different aspects of the position of young people in the employment system of European countries. Written by an international team of authors, the chapters provide unique inter-country and inter-system comparisons. The contributors see the problem mainly in terms of a mismatch between aspirations, expectations and qualifications of young people and their employment possibilities. They examine the manifestations of this mismatch in different countries, and explore different approaches to the problem, focusing on trends in education and employment, changes in values, orientations and preferences, and institutional regulations related to the transition from school to work.

International and interdisciplinary in its approach, the book makes an important contribution to the better understanding of a major social phenomenon.

The Editors
Wladyslaw Adamski is a Professor at the Institute of Sociology and Philosophy, Polish Academy of Sciences, Warsaw. Peter Grootings is a Project Director at the European Centre for the Development of Vocational Training (Cedefop), Berlin.

Youth, Education and Work in Europe

Edited by

Wladyslaw Adamski

and

Peter Grootings

for the European Co-ordination Centre for Research and
Documentation in Social Sciences

London and New York

First published 1989
by Routledge
11 New Fetter Lane, London EC4P 4EE

Simultaneously published in the USA and Canada
by Routledge
a division of Routledge, Chapman and Hall, Inc.
29 West 35th Street, New York, NY 10001

Reprinted 1990

© 1989 European Co-ordination Centre for Research and Development
in Social Sciences

Printed in Great Britain by
Antony Rowe Ltd, Chippenham, Wiltshire

British Library Cataloguing in Publication Data

Youth, education and work in Europe
  1. Europe. Young Persons. Employment
  I. Adamski, Wladyslaw II. Grootings,
  Peter, *1951*– III. European Co-ordination
  Centre for Research and Documentation in
  Social Sciences
  331.3'4'094

  ISBN 0-415-00578-7

Library of Congress Cataloging in Publication Data

Youth, education, and work in Europe.
  1. Youth-Employment-Europe. 2. Education–
Economic aspects–Europe. 3. Occupational
training–Europe. I. Adamski, Wladyslaw. II. Grootings,
Peter, 1951– . III. European Co-ordination Centre
for Research and Documentation in Social Sciences.
HD6276.E8Y7 1989 331.3'4'094   88-32549

ISBN 0-415-00578-7

Contents

Tables

Figures

Preface

The chapters contained in this book present some of the results of a project that has been quite unique in a number of respects. Researchers from several East and West European countries have worked together during several years to discuss a problem which they have considered to be a crucial one in their countries: the transition from school to work.

At a series of meetings in different European places each of them has presented the outcomes of the research done in their countries, and has tried to explain their situation as well as to understand that of the others. Needless to say that these meetings have been interesting, stimulating, and, above all, always dominated by an atmosphere of intellectual 'glasnost' and personal friendship.

This book, in many ways, shows only a small part of what has been achieved. In our view, however, this is quite sufficient to legitimate the publication. The various chapters document in a double sense the results of our work. Each of them is based on a comparative analysis of one aspect of the larger problem in a number of countries (but always East-West countries) and illustrates the attempt to understand the specificities of youth employment problems.

Each chapter has been written by an international group of authors and thus illustrates the cooperative nature of our work. The reader who is acquainted with international comparative research will understand the many problems of principle and practice involved in this type of project. We have gone through all of them and we are all aware that we have not yet solved them. However, we are confident to have made a valuable contribution and many of us have continued to work together on the basis of these first results.

One set of problems of this type of work has been solved to our full satisfaction, i.e. the preparation for final publication of manuscripts originating from various countries.

We are extremely happy that we have had the assistance of some highly qualified colleagues: Monica Emmer, who did the linguistic editing, and Joanna Ambrus, who has taken care not only of all the word processing for this book but also helped us with the organisation of our research meetings. Waltraud Salimi has typed several versions of chapters.

While the present book contains comparative chapters, a second book, also to be published in this series, will be devoted to national analyses of the transition from school to work in the countries that have participated in the project.

Wladyslaw Adamski
Peter Grootings

1

Transition from School to Work. Introduction

Wladyslaw Adamski, Peter Grootings and Fred Mahler

Introduction

Young people have always moved between scepticism, high expectations and realism when it comes to judging the position and role of youth in society. And there is no exception for those who study the problems of youth. While the student revolts of the 1960s in the Western countries came as unexpectedly to most researchers of youth (Rosenmayr, 1972) as the resurgence of class conflicts came to most sociologists of work (Crouch and Pizzorno, 1978), after an initial phase of excessive expectations and a relatively long period of economic crises, the growing realism of social scientists manifested itself in attempts to combine the expectations of the 1960s with both the reality of the present and the possibilities of the future. This has had interesting implications for theory and research and also has led to the emergence of a specific field of study: the transition from school to work. This transition from school to work can be regarded as an adequate synthesis formulation for the major problems that youth are momentarily facing with respect to their integration into the employment system and into society at large. At the same time the increased problems that now occur in the transition from school to work have led to a rethinking of the concept of youth (the stage of life in the transition from adolescence to adulthood) among youth researchers in at least two ways: not only students but also the young working class (employed or unemployed) have become an object of study (Adamski, 1983b); secondly, it has been realised that the transition from school to work is only one aspect of the more general transition from adolescence to adulthood, and that it is closely connected with another transition which is taking place at the same time, i.e. the transition from the parental family to

1

independent forms of living (see e.g. Andics, 1983; Galland, 1985). It seems though that the sociology of youth is quite helpless in dealing alone with this topic. As a matter of fact the issue is not restricted to this discipline and one can, indeed, discover a fortunate development from a discipline-oriented approach to a problem-oriented one in many research projects integrating the input and cooperation of various other disciplines. While obviously the study of the transition from school to work has to rely at least on such disciplines as demography, sociology of education, sociology of youth, sociology of work (labour market, work organisation, industrial relations) and of social stratification, in this paper we shall have to limit ourselves mainly to analysing a number of developments in the sociology of education, youth and work. While these disciplines have studied many other issues besides the transition from school to work, only those developments will be looked at which have special relevance for our topic. With respect to the sociology of work, it will be mainly its attempts to explain the development of the employment structure at the level of work organisations that are of interest. These attempts are characterised by the search for more social explanations and a growing withdrawal from the traditional technological-deterministic approach. In the field of sociology of youth and education, our main point of interest is also the development of less deterministic approaches. An additional limitation is the focus on trends which have an international comparative perspective, in particular, on comparative research in, and between, Eastern and Western Europe.

Youth theory and research

Youth and crisis

Social scientists' preoccupation with youth is characterised by a new attitude. In the late 1960s, hopes and optimism resulting from student protests prevailed over the fears and restraints; in recent decades, however, publications have not only become more moderate - even pessimistic - but also more deeply rooted in the fundamentals of empirical fact and theoretical thinking. It is sufficient to look at the constantly changing notion of what researchers mean by youth to appreciate the depth of this change.

It was Kenniston (1971) who introduced to experimental

psychology at the beginning of the seventies a separate 'just emerging' stage of life that he called 'youth'. He suggested reserving the concept of youth for students and former students, mainly of middle class origin, between the ages of eighteen and thirty. Before him, the concept of youth was nothing more than a substitute for adolescents, i.e. for those teenagers staying at school. A further extension of the youth category subsequently took place. The word came to embrace both dropouts from school and those excluded from the labour market (especially in the developed Western societies) as well as the increasing number of young people already gainfully employed but still far from achieving the social independence characteristic of full adulthood. The latter tendency seems to be more clearly the case in the East European socialist societies.

This shift in attention has led to defining youth as 'a socially extended or prolonged stage of life'. Such a definition in turn is not only grounded in the changed positions of young people in a period of economic crisis, but also has made it possible to expand on the traditional areas of youth research (age segregation through the school system, youth culture, student protest) and to include additional issues such as unemployment or underemployment; lack of economic security; and the exclusion from active, socially responsible or rewarding professional and civic roles both within and outside the workplace. One general trend, which can be observed when evidence from this research is put together, indicates that contemporary youth tends to occupy a less important or even 'marginal' status *vis-à-vis* society. In reaction to this observed marginalisation, some researchers have elaborated on more general theories. These also include the reverse trend of a 'juvenisation of society' which is understood as a process dialectically connected with 'youth's socialisation or integration into society' and 'youth's marginalisation from society' (Mitev, 1980; Mahler, 1983a). Contrary to the period when the 'youth culture' prevailed, present day researchers are also more inclined to identify and locate the causes of youth marginalisation not so much (or no longer only) in the family or in educational institutions but primarily in the area of work and its broader socio-political dimensions (Adamski, 1983b; UNESCO, 1979, 1981; OECD, 1980, 1984; CEDEFOP, 1981; CERI, 1983; Baethge, 1984; Grootings, 1984a; Mitev *et al.*, 1983b; Hartmann, 1984).

Main concepts and theoretical approaches in youth studies

Youth culture approach

As a product of technological and structural changes brought about by industrialisation, and particularly by one of its attendant developments, i.e. the school segregation of larger age-cohorts, the concept of youth culture has emerged and still continues to flourish primarily in the more developed countries. The typical youth culture approach involves a preoccupation with the specific problems confronting teenagers, those confronting peer groups at school or university, and those arising from cultural norms and patterns of behaviour. Since the early 1960s, when James J. Coleman (1961) published his now classic 'The adolescent society', the youth culture concept seems to have remained basically unchanged. Introspection, psychological attachment to peers, concern for the 'underdog' and interest in change - all these characteristics have preserved their validity. Critics (for details of the debate see Kreutz, 1974; Rosenmayr, 1976) argue that the social background of young people - even in American high schools - is too differentiated to allow classification of youth as a homogeneous social group with its own culture. Research has also shown that when individuals choose peers, self-selective mechanisms operate, leading to the selection of friends with similar social backgrounds. The youth culture concept is, as Kreutz (1974) pointed out, still theoretically controversial. Moreover, the shift in attention towards youth outside the schools has also had some implications. In the face of high youth unemployment, the issue of the relationship between 'unemployment culture' and youth culture has again been raised (UNESCO, 1985b). The questions which are relevant here are whether and to what extent young, unemployed people are basically in the same situation as unemployed adults, or whether their situation has some special characteristics (Kreutz and Wuggenig, 1978). At least two aspects have to be taken into account in this respect. The one is that youth unemployment usually occurs when the individual has left school and is looking for his first - acceptable - job. Young people in this situation still have access to their previous peer groups; especially in areas with high overall unemployment, such peer groups could continue to exist among unemployed youth, receiving a new quality in terms of solidarity or as a specific organisational form for resistance against 'institutionalised subordination' (Starr, 1981). Other research, however, does point at processes of isolation occurring among young unemployed people, similar to those which adults experience (Marsden and Duff, 1975; Wacker, 1978; Heinemann, 1978; Taylor, 1983; Alaluf *et al.* 1983). The second aspect which characterises youth unemployment is that it occurs in a very specific period in a person's life, creating not only a massive break in the socialisation process with potential consequences for the development of the individual personality (Heinemann, 1978; Baethge, 1984), but also causing considerable difficulties for those individuals trying to break away from the parental family and establish their independence (Galland, 1985). Again, however, research has stressed the fundamental heterogeneity of the youth category, both in terms of the objective employment situation, which has also become more diverse through various state youth employment measures (Köditz, 1981), and in terms of the social class background and the different support and solidarity strategies offered by the parental family (Baethge *et al.* 1983; Galland and Louis, 1984; Galland, 1985). It has been signalled many times, though, that there is a great lack of research on how young people actually are coping with employment problems. It can be seriously questioned, however, whether the youth culture concept is, indeed, still of great value for answering this question. Certainly in the socialist countries it has not received influential intellectual status.

Counterculture and post-materialist life orientations

Another product of Western affluence and segregationism is the concept of counterculture. Despite its failure to fulfil the most radical prophecies, it has gained a great deal of public attention on both sides of the political spectrum. Support from the left came for the explicit criticism of extremely individualistic and materialistic patterns of the dominant culture as well as for the appeal to the young generation to change the status quo (Marcuse, 1964). For the right, the same phenomena functioned as warnings of dangerous trends in society (Inglehart, 1977). While the times are over in which youth, simply taken as an age-group, could be regarded as a factor of social change just because of its 'youthfulness' (Hübner-Funk, 1983), one cannot deny that the counterculture has been partially successful in formulating and shaping alternatives, transforming behaviours and policies and even in challenging existing social institutions. In the field of youth research, the counterculture has also meant a greater attention to the realm of values. Relevant in the present context is the debate about changed or changing work values (see Comte, 1983; Baethge, 1984; Grootings, 1984a; Wilpert, 1984). Inglehart's thesis (1977) of a noticeable change in value orientations between the generations (from materialist to post-materialist) has received much attention, but has also been criticised heavily both on theoretical (confusion of intra- and inter-cohort changes) and methodological grounds (reliance on single-item survey research, see Baethge *et al.*, 1983). Contrary to the 'silent revolution' (Inglehart, 1977) or the 'value disintegration' (Noelle-Neumann, 1978) in which work is losing its central meaning among youth, recent studies have rather convincingly pointed at quite another development, common in both East and West European countries. Due to structural changes in the socialisation process (longer schooling, stabilisation of societal developments), the younger generation has developed higher aspirations and expectations towards work. In this respect, the relevant issue is not so much youth's escape from work but rather the *mismatch* between aspirations, expectations and qualifications of the younger generations on the one hand and the employment possibilities presently open to them on the other. Such a definition of the problem necessarily leads to the study of the transition from school to work as the main period (life stage) when young people are confronted with this mismatch. It also leads the sociology of youth to include the first years of working life and to make use of the knowledge of other disciplines (sociology of education, sociology of work). We shall return to these issues later.

Generation and life-course approaches

While the concept of generation is an old one, a relatively new aspect in youth sociology is the attempt to relate a given age cohort (generation) of newcomers in a society with its own specific cultural and historical development. Margaret Mead's concept of a 'generation gap' (1970), as both an unavoidable outcome of technological development and at the same time a creative factor of cultural and social change, has been criticised among others for emphasising too strongly the pressures and requirements that new technologies would impose on inter-generational relations and for underestimating the fact that older generations would effectively resist serious changes in traditionally established patterns. The process of family change, with the young generation as its dynamic component, would be better analysed if it were taken as an independent variable *vis-à-vis* the external environment and not made wholly dependent on such macro processes as industrialisation and urbanisation. A life-cycle or life-course perspective, by distinguishing different time dimensions, opens an interesting approach to research in this respect. One of the advocates of this orientation in American sociology presents this approach as follows:

> Life course is conceptualised in terms of the sociology of age and its multiple meanings. Data on age locates individuals according to: 1/ developmental stage in the aging process; 2/ life stage in the sequential pattering of social roles and options; and 3/ historical context, with its implications for cohort membership and opportunities. Age locates individuals in the social structure through age-related normative criteria and in historically specific cohorts by year of birth. Within the perspective of social change and continuity, the processes of socialisation and role allocation (e.g., from school to job, etc.) serve to articulate people and social options in the course of aging and cohort succession. Cohorts that are differentiated by social change, size, and composition establish different contexts of socialisation and life opportunity, a point most graphically illustrated by relatively small cohorts that come of age during a period of rising prosperity and large cohorts that enter adulthood at a time of economic hardship. Members of a cohort also tend to vary on exposure to particular change events (such as rising education and employment among women), and this difference leads to life course variations within successive cohorts. In both inter-cohort and intra-cohort approaches, the first task is to specify how historical conditions interact with the human biography to alter the course and psychology of lives (Elder, 1975).

Considering the usefulness of family studies for understanding the role of the younger generation in contemporary societies, it seems particularly relevant whether the intra-family mechanisms of the transmission of basic needs, values and aspirations function in such a way that children become a kind of replica of their parents or not (or, to put it in more general terms, that the intra-family mechanisms function in such a way that younger generations are a mere reproduction of their parents' generation or not). It is, of course, stratification and mobility research which gives strong evidence for the reproduction thesis, be it modified by educational levels. Yet, the life-course approach would add to the stratification structure the analysis of a) the specific features of the developmental stage of society at which the decisive phase of socialisation of a given generation takes place and b) the distinctive features of a given socio-political system and the types of culture and ideology that are dominant in it. When dealing with youth's employment problems, this approach therefore would stress the specificities of a post-war crisis generation in different socio-economic systems (Morgan, 1975; Adamski, 1983b). Moreover, it would also claim that the employment situation, i.e. the transition from school to work, cannot be isolated from other basic characteristics associated with the period of youth, especially the transition from the parental family to independent forms of living (Galland, 1985).

Youth as an integral and differentiated component of social structures: aspirations vs. their fulfilment

Typical of this approach is to see youth, or the young 'ascending' generations, as belonging to historically determined types of social classes, and/or ethnic, cultural and socio-professional categories. Contrary to traditional youth-culture research, those youth who are school dropouts are also included, as well as those looking for steady employment or those who have already entered the labour force and set up their own families but still are far from fully integrated into society. This approach puts - in contrast to biological, psychological and psycho-analytical concepts - an emphasis on the objective social conditions in which the whole process of education and socialisation of a particular generation takes place. The predominant type of economy and technology of production, the nature of the socio-political structures and the place reserved for the 'ascending' generation in this pattern are usually taken to be 'conditions' in order for youth to have a real chance to play an active role or not. This role involves not only shaping one's own destiny through the processes of adaptation but also, at the same time, adapting the inherited state of cultural and social relations in accordance with new aspirations. Problems may arise when the young generation's new aspirations (resulting from structural changes in the process of socialisation, Baethge, 1984) clash with the opportunities that are offered by social and

8

economic structures.

A well-developed way of investigating this problem is to look at vocational aspirations and the chances of their fulfilment as measured by actual vocational choice (e.g. Shubkin, 1984; Holsinger, 1978; Diederen, 1981). A second research perspective within the structural approach, which until now has hardly taken place in empirical research, presents itself when we trace further the contradictions in youth's aspirations and their structural constraints: what are the possibilities of young people to 'adapt' the unfavourable environment to their vocational, cultural and socio-political aspirations? This brings the question of power and interest organisation to youth research. While it has been generally recognised that youth as such lacks the organisational structures to form an effective force and that they - as newcomers - are systematically confronted with structures of vested interests which are difficult to overcome, the forms of adaptation typically investigated are mainly individual or collective withdrawals. Recent research into attitudes and behaviour of young unemployed, however, gives a much more heterogeneous picture. Depending on social class background and aspirations ('life projects'), young people react and cope quite differently with unemployment (Galland and Louis, 1984). The question arises as to whether and under which conditions the 'unfavourable environment' could be changed through innovative attitudes and behaviour in the labour market and at the workplace. It is at this very point that industrial and work sociology has shown, for instance, a certain convergence of interests (for quite different reasons) between certain groups of youth with rather instrumental work and working-time attitudes and enterprises that are aiming at flexible work organisation and labour force structures in the present phase of rationalisation. Similarly, under conditions of a simultaneous lack of labour force and higher educational levels, we have witnessed serious attempts by enterprises to develop 'alternative forms of work organisation' in order to respond to the 'new' work aspirations and expectations of the young labour force (Cooper and Mumford, 1979; IILS, 1978, 1983; ILO, 1979, Grootings and Stefanov, 1985a).

This perspective basically leads one to accept that there are still unexplored possibilities for fulfilling youth's aspirations - if taken seriously - by applying a model of socio-political adaptation to society, which refuses the total acceptance of well-established norms and offers instead a creative, constructive model of 'selective and dynamic social adaptation' (Adamski, 1983b; Fragnière and Doorten, 1984). Attempts to develop a new paradigm of thinking based on these ideas have been developed, in particular by youth researchers from the socialist countries (see Mahler, 1983b; Mitev *et al.* 1983b; and Adamski, 1983c).

Sociology of work and technology

Two paradigms

The sociology of youth has developed fruitful attempts and approaches to the study of the development of the young generation's own aspirations and expectations towards work and that generation's incidence with a specific stage in the life-course as well as its relations with the specific socio-historical development of societies with their own social, economic and political characteristics. Above all, however, it has - as manifested in attempts to develop paradigms around 'juvenisation' and 'juvenology' - contributed to taking such 'new' aspirations and expectations seriously, both as products of societal socialisation processes themselves and as potential factors of social change. At the same time, though, the sociology of youth has not been very successful - and sometimes quite unrealistic - in assessing the actual existing possibilities for the realisation of such aspirations: mainly because it has, so far, not seriously incorporated the study of the realm of work into its analysis. Sociology of youth has oscillated between voluntaristic optimism and technological and economic, deterministic pessimism. The questions that have to be posed now are what the sociology of work can say about actual developments in the world of work, about the impact of technological change and - finally - about the degrees of freedom for human intervention.

Child (1986) has pointed out that the situation confronting any discussion of research on technology and work in the western social sciences is one of great diversity in the specific conceptualisation and operationalisation of technology. It is therefore important in any assessment of studies on technology and work to keep this diversity of conceptual and operational definitions in mind. This being the case, one can distinguish two major approaches to the relationship between technology and work:

- a technological-deterministic tradition
- social analyses of technology and work.

The main issue that both approaches address themselves to is the question, Does technology shape social and economic organisation or do social and economic organisation shape technology? While authors like Marglin (1976), who take the second position, relate this question mainly to intra-organisational relations in capitalist societies, the question has become increasingly topical for international and inter-system comparisons as well (Grootings, 1986a).

The technological-deterministic approach

The technological-deterministic approach is the traditional one. Widely adopted, although mostly in an implicit way, in practically all research done about the relationship between technology and work until the seventies (for reviews see Maurice, 1980; Child, 1986), it maintains that technology has necessary implications for work in terms of determining the level and structure of employment, the nature and experience of work and work organisation. In fact, there are two aspects to this position. First of all, it is assumed that, from a strategic point of view, enterprises will have to adopt the latest technology sooner or later in order to secure continued business viability. Technology will therefore spread more or less automatically. Second, on the operational level, it is assumed that once a given technology has been introduced it will have predictable and necessary consequences. In other words, there is one best way, or at least one optimal way, of applying a given technology (Kerr *et al.*, 1973). In social science studies in the West this approach is connected with a view of technology as a neutral force for progress, technology being the result of advancement in science. While such a view of technology is also present in the East European socialist countries (Richta, 1969), it has been stressed there that the social consequences depend on the socio-economic system characteristics of societies. The results of science are to be used differently, i.e. unplanned or planned, and based on different criteria in capitalist and socialist countries. In most of the empirical research done at the enterprise and workplace level, however, a firm technological-deterministic approach has been applied as Kulpinska (1986) has shown in a review of East European research. In most cases, technology, as in western research, has been taken as the independent variable, and one has looked for the implications and consequences of its introduction and use. The consequences are seen to lie both in the quantity and the quality of employment. While the issue of the quantitative relationship between technological change and employment is so complex that clear predictions are very difficult to make, the belief that technology is related to the creation of 'structural unemployment' has received strong support from various sides (Rothwell and Zegveld, 1979). For Marxists, the objective role of technology is to cheapen the cost of production and to replace the labour force (see most recently, e.g. Schaff, 1985). Neo-classical theory sees increases in unemployment to be a consequence of shifts of labour from stagnant growth sectors to technologically based ones. Others have regarded technology as such to be the basic cause of structural unemployment. While this field of research is vast, and opinions still differ widely, it has now become generally accepted now that an adequate analysis of the relationship between technology and employment would have to take into account both macro-economic variables and individual features of specific industries and organisations (Child, 1986).

A whole body of research is now available, part of which was initially based, in its assumptions and design, on a technological-deterministic approach (e.g. Forslin *et al.*, 1979 and 1981) that has empirically shown a high variation in employment levels and employment structures as well as in workers' skills and attitudes connected with similar types of technology (Dore, 1973; Gallie, 1978; Maurice *et al.*, 1980; Maurice *et al.* 1982; Sorge *et al.*, 1981). In other words, technology can apparently be used in conjunction with policies to replace the employees' skills or to complement and enhance them. It has also been argued that employment structures (both at the national and at the enterprise level) have assumed an institutionalised form in terms of both occupational structures and classification systems which are created by educational systems and defended by industrial relations systems (Maurice *et al.*, 1982). Braverman (1974) has initiated a discussion known as the labour process debate (see Thompson, 1983) with his argument that it is management control as advocated in Taylorist work organisation, where technology is a mere instrument, that explains the development of employment structures (deskilling). A further example is the socio-technical systems approach, which has argued that a given technology allows a choice for economically viable alternative designs of work organisation and that the optimal design would have to take note of workers' interests as well (Butera and Thurman, 1984). These strands of research, however different they may be, have all contributed to a shift in attention from technology *per se* towards the 'organisation of work'. Developments in work that have previously been regarded as more or less direct consequences of technological change are now seen to be the result of work organisational measures (Lutz, 1984). Research subsequently has focused on those forces which influence developments in work organisation, of which technology is only one.

If we look at work organisation as an institutionalised form of (horizontal and vertical) division of labour, then some implications of this shift in research approach (which of course can only be sketched here along very general lines) for an understanding of the labour market chances for young people become clear. First of all, basic premises of technology assessment and of educational planning based on it have become obsolete. It is no longer possible to study some typical examples of different levels of technological development and to generalise towards tendencies of human labour from these findings. The enterprise, where employment is created, can no longer be treated as a black box (see also Little, 1986). Given the historical interrelationships between educational systems and patterns of work organisation (Lutz, 1976; Maurice *et al.*, 1982), youth unemployment can also no longer be regarded *only* as an educational problem: work organisations have been shown to adapt to the labour market structures produced by the educational system. In principle, therefore, higher qualifications and different expectations towards (content and conditions of) work can be integrated into organisational designs. Actually, this has been the case in some Western and East European socialist countries during periods of high labour shortage. There are, however, limits set for a too high voluntarism, and these are basically of three kinds:

-   the character and the organisation of the social relations of production (mode of production);
-   the character and the organisation of relations in production (the labour process);
-   the general state of the economy, or more concretely, the market position of enterprises.

The second approach, which we now turn to, can be characterised as the attempt to study technology and work within this social context.

Societal analyses of technology and work

While the search for a new paradigm is present, there is no consensus yet about any alternative paradigm. As a matter of fact, different approaches raise different arguments against technological determinism, and it is exactly because of this that it would be futile to expect a great consensus to be developed any time soon. However, since the sharing of a paradigm, even a negative one, can be considered to be a necessary condition for fruitful communication, cooperation and even comparison, it is relevant to look in more detail at the various perspectives and to see on which points they might eventually be compatible.

It is interesting to note, as was pointed out by Lutz (1984), that many researchers who actually started their research on the basis of the main premises of technological determinism were forced to change their views because the different case studies undertaken by them did not show identical and direct relationships between technology and work. This has generally forced them to accept the existence of some kind of flexibility, located most of all in the organisation of work, as well as to look for other factors besides technology to explain the latter. International comparative research has greatly contributed to this line of argument. Various recent publications (Dore, 1973; Lutz, 1976; Gallie, 1978; Dubois and Makó, 1980; Sorge *et al.*, 1981; Maurice *et al.*, 1982) have shown that enterprises using a similar technology, but located in different countries, have different organisational, manning, and qualification structures. These enterprises also employ workers whose attitudes and behaviour differ considerably. From such studies we know about the relevance of specific societal characteristics for shaping work organisation. Such characteristics have been located mainly in structures and developments of educational and industrial relations systems. Burawoy (1985) also showed the relevance of political conditions for factory regimes under capitalism and socialism. More generally, these societal conditions are located at two levels: at the enterprise level and at the level of society. It is in the importance given to either level as well as in the interpretation of the relationships between the two (micro-macro; enterprise and society) that the various approaches within this 'societal type of analysis' differ from one another.

One classic approach argues against technological determinism that technology itself is nothing but the materialisation of specific values, images and interests and that it is the latter that therefore determine the consequences of its development, introduction and use (Noble, 1979). If the values and images of technical designers, which now typically aim at the elimination of human labour, could be changed (Rosenbrock, 1983), or if workers' points of view and interests would also be taken into account through participative models of design and implementation (Andersen *et al.*, 1979), the technology would look different and its impact on work would be different as well (Hirschhorn, 1984; Shaiken, 1984).

Another position maintains that it is not so much technology *per se*, but rather the socio-economic context of the society, that determines the impact of technology. The same technology would have a different impact when used under socialist or under capitalist conditions. Private or state ownership of the means of production relate technology to different aims and goals of production and offer possibilities for a different use of technology (Richta, 1969). A similar argument can be found among some western Marxists who point out that in the capitalist system it ultimately is the surplus value creation by exploitation of labour - for which technology is an instrument (of intensification and control) - that shape production relations. Both technology and work organisation are aspects of a continuous rationalisation drive. Even when there are choices for alternative work organisation available, that form will be 'chosen' which best guarantees the capitalists' interests (Wilkinson, 1983; Brandt *et al.*, 1978).

Another point to take into account is that some early participants in the debate initiated by the publication of Braverman's *Labour and Monopoly Capital* (1974) looked at technology as an instrument for (better) control over and (more) deskilling of the labour force by capitalist management (Zimbalist, 1979). Contrary to such unilateral control arguments, more recent publications from this debate tend to look at technology and the organisation of work as the outcome of conflicts and interest struggles between different groups of management and workers (Edwards, 1979; Burawoy, 1985; Kern and Schumann, 1984; Makó, 1986).

Yet another group of authors argues that the present new technologies (especially micro-electronics technology) have specific new characteristics that distinguish them fundamentally from previous generations of technology and that this would account for an even greater potential of flexibility (Lutz, 1984; Gustavsen, 1984; Lojkine, 1982; Butera and Thurman, 1984). Such qualities as their relative cheapness, compactness, reliability, accuracy, speed and low energy use have increased the practical possibilities of their application, especially for small-scale use. Changed market conditions, asking for flexible and adaptable production structures and demanding quality rather than quantity as well as the availability of high numbers of highly qualified labour, have created the favourable conditions for the increased introduction of these factors. Others, however, argue that exactly because of the flexibility of the new technologies, they become aspects of organisation technology themselves, and in becoming an integral part of rationalisation strategies will therefore lead in the long run to less variation in work organisation (Benz-Overhage *et al.*, 1982). In a similar vein, but at another level of analysis, Maurice and his colleagues hypothesise that the flexibility of new technologies will make it easier to integrate them into the existing institutional frameworks and national traditions and that they, therefore, could lead to an accentuation of existing trends and differences rather than to fundamental changes or convergence (Eyraud *et al.*, 1984).

In organisational studies, it has been the growing criticism against traditional quantitative, comparative, structural and contingency approaches which has led to what Lammers (1983) calls 'the fifth phase': the study of the relations between organisation and society (see also Lammers and Hickson, 1979; Kudera, 1977; Zey-Ferrel and Aiken, 1981; Mrela and Kostecki, 1981). As opposed to a 'culture free' approach, these studies increasingly analyse organisations in their cultural setting (values and institutions) as 'cultured organisations' (Sorge, 1980). While these approaches can take account of the various differences in organisational structures that especially international comparative research has revealed, the relationship between the organisation and society has, as Maurice *et al.* (1982) stress, often been analysed in a rather mechanistic and one-sided way: the organisation as influenced by its external environment. Maurice and his colleagues pay attention to the analysis of the *relationships* between the enterprise (and its main social actors) and society by looking at the very processes (socialisation and organisation) that not only produce the social actors but also the 'space' in which they relate to each other.

It is true that the research directions sketched here tend to focus on explaining the characteristics and development of work organisations in terms of more qualitative dimensions, while the more quantitative aspects are, to a certain extent, beyond their scope. Nevertheless, they contribute greatly to our knowledge about the factual interrelations between enterprise and labour market structures (as produced by educational systems and organised in and by industrial relations systems) and about the decisive role of 'political' processes (of bargaining and control) inside the enterprise. It is within this complex context that one could study the position of school leavers (with different types and levels of qualification) on the labour market and in the work organisation. It has to be added here that while we now have many studies documenting the increasing structural lability and marginalisation (Baethge *et al.*, 1980) of youth on the labour market[1], studies on changing employment conditions in the enterprises are still missing. We have now touched upon the relationship between the employment system and the system of education several times. In the next section we shall concentrate explicitly on some of those developments in the sociology of education which are relevant for our discussion.

Sociology of education

Education and work: unilateral determinism or reciprocal relationships?

When considering the common issues of sociology of youth, education and work there is one question which we can consider as a central one: is education determined by work (and should it be so) or is it better to recognise and to argue for a reciprocal relationship between the two?

Many modern answers to this question argue that since school has to prepare young people for (working) life, education ceases to be autonomous, with its own goals, functions, structures and processes and becomes a mere tool for labour integration and manpower reproduction. Within the theoretical approaches to education and schooling, we can therefore discover a primary tendency which emphasises the deterministic influence of the economy on education (or, to put it another way, of work on

17

schooling). An intermediate position stresses the total isolation, the 'insularity', of both education and work as subsystems of the social system as a whole. At the extreme opposite pole of the continuum, we can find the argument for an autonomous position of education and even the thesis that it is the school system which is determining social development. And, we can find a position which underlines the interrelationships between the school and work systems, the mutual influencing of education and work.

It is possible to visualise these different relationships between education and work, as follows:

Education		Work	
⇐	I	⇒	- overdeterminism of education by work
⇐	II	⇒	- autonomous development of school-work
⇐	III	⇒	- overdeterminism of work by education
⇐	IV	⇒	- reciprocal influence

While pre-industrial societies promoted, in educational theory and practice, mainly the relative autonomous position (II) and, in the utopian and romantic pedagogics, even an overdeterminism of work by the school system and of society by education (III), modern societies have reversed this trend: they stress the determinism of school by work and of education by economy (I). However, a growing awareness of the misfortunes of education and labour within such overdeterministic tendencies - which resulted *inter alia* in a mismatch between schooling and working - raised many critical issues against this trend. It is worthwhile to correlate this new antideterministic tendency (IV) within the sociology of education with similar developments in the field of sociology of work and technology and with those theories of youth which stress youth's active, creative, and emancipatory role in society. Let us first, however, have a closer look at some recent developments in the sociology of education that are relevant to the issue of transition from school to work.

Sociology of education and transition from school to work

Within the large range of different approaches that have relevance for the transition problematic, two main paradigms can be distinguished: the first stresses the equilibrium, the mutual consensus and the importance of exogenous features in the relationship among education and society and attributes to youth's transition a merely instrumental role; the second one stresses the changes, conflicts and endogenous features in this relationship and assigns a new role to youth's transition aimed at contributing to the changing relationship among education, work and society. Within these two paradigms, there are at least four main theoretical approaches in which one can summarise the existing methods for analysing the transition from school to work.

As part of the first paradigm, there is one influential approach which describes education in terms of its formative finality and efficiency, treats it as economic capital, and treats school as human investment, arguing that education's main task is to prepare the labour force by providing vocational and scientific training. The main goal of the educational process is - from the point of view of this approach - learning; the ideal personality is the cultivated man; main school activities are the development of vocational and scientific skills, cognitive development and knowledge accumulation. The educational process is centred on intellectual education, schooling is characterised by a dual system with a separation of elementary/vocational education from secondary/higher education. Unequal access opportunities, school careers and status positions are due to selection procedures based on social inequalities. Theory is separate from practice; the curriculum is divided into subjects, with directive pedagogy and post-figurative relations (from adults to youth) emphasising individual performance as the main evaluation criterion. Its immediate output is the accumulation of knowledge and skills and its long-term output is to meet labour market requirements while preserving the existing hierarchy in the social division of labour.

As a consequence, transition from school to work is seen merely as an *'adaptative'* process correlated with the traditional features of the school system - separated in space and time from the employment system and from society as a whole. This approach stresses the instrumental role of the transition process as something which responds to the needs of the employment system.

Without ignoring its positive traits, we may conclude that this approach corresponds at best with the conformistic, paternalistic and alienating approach of youth and with the technological deterministic orientation in work research.

As part of the same paradigm, a second approach sees socialisation as the main goal of education. This approach studies education in terms of symbolic (cultural) capital, defines school as a transmitter of values (of 'role-learning'), and defines the essential function of school as the imparting of values and norm-abiding attitudes. For this approach the ideal personality is the moral man. While the structure of the schooling system is characterised by a common body in the first stage (it is only at a later stage that a separation in two streams without reciprocal communication occurs and the selection procedures aim at equal access and developing relatively homogeneous groups), it preserves at the same time unequal opportunities, school careers and status ascriptions at the macro level. The structure of the schooling system also emphasises formative psycho-social subjects within the curricula: the schooling relations are viewed as a combination of directive and non-directive pedagogics and emphasis is put on small group evaluation criteria like social identity. It considers education as a dependent variable of the social ethos, whereby school has as its main output the adaptation of young people to the existing axiological system, including the system's work value orientations, mainly through integrative procedures at the macro level.

Thus, according to this *'micro-integrative'* theory, transition from school to work is an instrument for the reproduction of the *status quo* (also specific for the first paradigm); however, the emphasis on micro factors and group interaction, on interdependencies of the social actors and on the mediation of objective values by cultural and moral pressures confers to this approach a better understanding of youth's transition as compared with the previous one. In this view, transition means professional and moral socialisation of young people for their future occupational and social integration; while the process continues to be insulated inside the school, some windows open toward social reality. The emerging anticipatory socialisation (learning and education in school for future life tasks) therefore, in the end, means nothing more than to adapt youth both to present and future requirements and constraints.

As part of the second paradigm, the *'macro-interrogative'*

theory views education as a variable dependent on the evolution of socio-economic and vocational structures of the respective society. The main goal of the schooling system, considered in terms of social capital, is professional mobility. The main functions of the schooling system are: professional development, stimulation of individual praxis-relevant capacities, socio-professional selection and promotion centred on know-how. The schooling system within this approach emphasises knowledge that will be useful in working life, natural sciences and technological subjects in the curricula and takes professional, theoretical and practical performance as evaluation criteria. Changes in the structure of the school are oriented towards bringing together learning and working while keeping them separate (experiments with learning by doing). The structure of the school stimulates increased individual mobility without alteration of unequal social structures and it promotes configurative relations (mutually from youth to adult). This, together with the development of actional capacities of the young, accentuates the changed perspective announced by this new approach in education.

In fact, some important consequences for the understanding and shaping of the transition process are arising from this approach: in the second paradigm, transition is viewed as a means for changing - through schooling, education and socialisation - the occupational status of social actors in the light of professional mobility. Education and schooling are still considered as dependent variables of the professional structure, yet this approach does give a more active role to education, i.e. to the learning process in school, which goes beyond a mere adaptive and conformistic integration of graduates in their jobs. In order to promote occupational mobility and professional competence, vocational education requires deep changes in the communication between the school and work organisations. The goal of good professional training within a perspective of full and efficient integration of young people in their future work, together with the claim for occupational mobility (even if this is of an individual kind and largely preserves social unequal structures), requires a reshapening of the transition process and asks for new education and social policies with regard to youth.

Such a *required change* to overcome the well-known drawbacks and contradictions is the common explicit objective of a number of theories and policies on schooling which could be included in a fourth approach: *structural change*. As part of the second paradigm, it stresses personality development and structural change as the main goals of education; education is seen as being dependent on socio-economic and political changes while also playing a role in structural changes. While the ideal personality from this new point of view is the specialist citizen, and the professional and political-moral man, this approach asserts the vocational and moral development of the personality as the main schooling functions, which implies a conscious and free participation of the individual. With regard to schooling structures, this approach aims to integrate school with practice and promotes recurrent education in the perspective of lifelong education. Consequently, the emphasis is on the *integration* of subjects in the curricula, an interdisciplinary approach to nature, man and society, non-directive pedagogics and pre-figurative relations (from youth to adult), while stimulating the self-development of an autonomous personality and its active participation in work and social affairs. In the light of the goal of equalisation of social statuses and increasing collective mobility, the selective procedures aim at equal access, opportunity, school careers and status ascriptions.

This approach creates new possibilities for the process of transition from school to work. In a relationship which avoids one-sided determinism by the economic or technological factor, the new features, goals, functions, contents and structures of schooling are intimately related to those of the employment system. The conformistic, adaptive and manipulative moulding of school leavers into 'eager tools' is transformed into an anticipatory emancipatory socialisation aiming at educating creative and autonomous personalities with authentic vocational and moral competences and participative attitudes.

Taking into account recent trends in the sociology of education, the study of transition from school to work would profit most from those approaches which not only recognise the necessary coping of education with technological, economic and social requirements as exogenous determinants but also stress the active role of education and of its endogenous factors of development. Such a perspective could allow for better contributions within the interdisciplinary approach of the transition problematic and for a more open view among researchers and policy makers with regard to the young generation's needs and aspirations. For example, the existing mismatch between aspirations and opportunities, between 'over'-education and occupational deskilling could stimulate other responses than the dominant technocratic one which argues, in an overdeterministic and paternalistic way, for the 'realistic' solution: the cooling down of youth's 'utopian' aspirations. It could instead lead to a search for changes in educational, work and macro-social structures which would aim for fulfilling youth's aspirations.

The transition from school to work: interdisciplinary and international research

Although it has not been possible to go into the details of the analysis of relevant theoretical developments here, it may be clear that there is some 'convergence' in the type of research questions and theoretical perspectives of the 'societal approaches' in the sociology of work, of the life-cycle and structural approaches in youth sociology and of the structural change theories in the sociology of education.

For the sociology of youth and education, it would be more fruitful to relate to the societal approaches in the sociology of work than to stick to traditional assumptions about the development of work and technology that are based on deterministic views. On the other hand, the sociology of work could be served very well by recent developments in the sociology of youth and sociology of education, especially when it comes to trying to understand the processes and mechanisms of the socialisation of young labour market entrants. Nevertheless, even if this were to already be the case, sociology of youth, education and work can only provide us with partial insights; important questions remain unanswered as long as no relations are established with additional relevant disciplines.

It is possible to schematise the development in these disciplines as follows:

	from overdeterminism	to anti-determinism
sociology of education	goals, functions, structure and curricula in schools are one-sided, determined by economic (work) pressures	goals, functions, structures and curricula in schools are mainly autonomous expressions of the reaction of the educational subsystem to the exogenous environmental pressures, including the economy
sociology of work	social division of work and work itself (job quality and work organisation) are technologically determined	social division of work and work organisation while being influenced by technology, have their own internal trends of development correlated with the social and cultural macro-context and its historical specific features
sociology of youth	social, labour and educational reproduction through youth's conformistic integration	social, labour and educational reproduction and change through emancipatory, anticipatory socialisation of youth and its social participation

The chapters that follow in this book are the result of an attempt to join the empirical and intellectual knowledge and experience of a wide group of social scientists. They not only come from different countries in Europe but also belong to different disciplines. Some members of this group have substantially contributed to the development of their respective disciplines, and all of them have been actively engaged in empirical research on the employment problems of youth in their own country. Each contributor also shares a preference for the anti-deterministic approaches within their disciplines as well as a desire to transcend narrow discipline-defined borders. What is presented here is the result of a rather unique international and interdisciplinary experiment in intellectual cooperation which has lasted for three years and which is to continue after the publication of this book. This expectation is grounded not only in the hope that colleagues who have become friends will stay in contact with each other, but also in the realisation that with our book we have only been able to make a very modest step towards a better understanding of a social phenomenon that is of more than intellectual interest. In fact, despite our different backgrounds, it has been our concern for the future of young generations and our engagement to contribute to a better world for them that has been the drive behind our cooperation.

The research project on Transition from School to Work in Europe[2] developed from an international conference held in Moscow (Winter 1983) on Attitudes and Behaviour of Youth Towards Work. The main conclusion from this conference was that it was not only the attitudes of young people that were changing (although some participants argued that no fundamental changes were taking place at all), but that there is a more complex situation of a growing mismatch between qualifications, expectations and aspirations of young people and job possibilities open to them (Grootings, 1984a).

It is this mismatch, experienced by young people as the transition from school to work, which was defined as a major social problem with which all European countries have to cope at present. It was agreed to devote a series of follow-up workshops to a comparative analysis of this problem. Researchers from fifteen European countries have been participating in this activity, with representatives from various international organisations taking part as observers.[3] From November 1984 on, a number of workshops have been organised with the support of participating teams. During this time, a stepwise strategy has been developed. In between these workshops, a small group, of changing composition, has met several times to steer the project. At the first workshop in Sofia, Bulgaria (Autumn 1984), national reports were presented giving an analysis of the Transition from School to Work problematic in the various European countries. For these reports a topic list was prepared so that all teams would cover comparable issues.[4] While it did not prove possible for all teams to furnish all the requested information, this topic list continues to function as our common frame of reference for all subsequent stages. The first meeting also helped us to determine what research (results) was available in the various countries and how the participating researchers approach the problematic. On the basis of this information, a programme for comparative analysis has been worked out which is characterised by its procedural nature and by a desire to relate the empirical analysis with the development of theory. Our work, therefore, has not been directly policy oriented.[5]

From a substantial point of view, these first contributions confirmed the validity of our hypothesis of the existence of transition problems in terms of a mismatch between aspirations, expectations and qualifications of young people and their employment possibilities. But in the different countries, the manifestations of this mismatch are different.

- While the main problem in the West is a shortage of employment, and for those who have employment a mismatch of qualifications, the problem in all socialist countries, is not the availability of working places (on the contrary), but rather of non-matching qualifications (underemployment), mainly in the newly industrialised countries. In Czechoslovakia and the German Democratic Republic, it appears that mismatches are also to be found on the level of non-qualification-related aspirations.
- In all countries similar developments have taken place in terms of the prolongation of compulsory education, the installment of higher educational levels and the increased numbers of better-qualified young people. Differences can be observed, however, in the relative emphasis put on general and vocational training.
- Countries have been differently affected by the consequences of recent economic crisis and the introduction of new technology.
- Countries also have followed different policies concerning the 'mismatches'; these have ranged from establishing closer links between education and work (and re-evaluating the status of vocational training) to an extension of the period of transition using a variety of measures.

At least three different approaches to these problems have been given by our participants:

- One mainly focuses on the school-and-work careers of individuals and includes issues like professional choice, mobility, prestige, etc. This approach also tends to locate the problems primarily within the educational domain, although some researchers do give attention to developments in the employment system.

- A second approach focuses more on education and work as societal subsystems with their own relative autonomy and on the different control mechanisms (market, planning) playing a role in the mutual adaptation of the two. Although certain educational reforms are thought to be necessary as well, the main focus seems to be put on the side of the employment system (employment and organisation strategies).

- A third approach opts for a more dynamic and prospective approach, taking into account changes in social content, meaning and the structure of education and work as such, due mainly to technological changes in the broadest sense of the word. Its focus was not so much on existing mismatches between education and work but on these phenomena as manifestations of the (necessary) development of new relationships.

The various national presentations also clearly show that a simple distinction between capitalist and socialist countries does not suffice to explain all the differences. A more detailed analysis of the dissimilarities in educational- and employment-opportunity systems is necessary. Such differences may cut across the socio-economic system differences as characterised by ownership relations and market-versus-planning. A more detailed analysis of the typical transition problems as they are manifested in the various countries is therefore necessary. This would also help clarify whether a number of the central concepts (like flexibility, disposability, marginalisation, precariousness) used in some of the national studies would refer to general phenomena or to specific societal developments characteristic for specific countries.

We decided to restrict our design to basically four dimensions that were relatively easy to describe:

- trends in education;
- trends in employment;
- changes in values, orientations and preferences;
- institutional regulations related to the transition from school to work.

And we elected to devote each subsequent workshop to a different type of analysis of these dimensions (see Figure 1.1).

Figure 1.1: Phases of the project Transition from School to Work in Europe

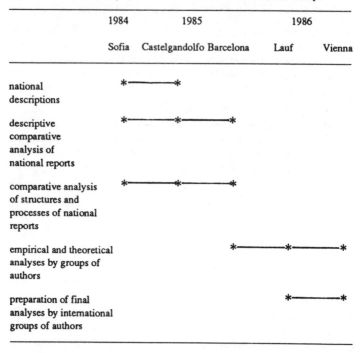

	1984	1985		1986	
	Sofia	Castelgandolfo	Barcelona	Lauf	Vienna
national descriptions	*———*				
descriptive comparative analysis of national reports	*———*	*———*			
comparative analysis of structures and processes of national reports	*———*	*———*			
empirical and theoretical analyses by groups of authors			*———*	*———*	*
preparation of final analyses by international groups of authors				*———*	

We shall be short about the contents and outcomes of the subsequent workshops since, once the foundations and working procedures were laid down, our work concentrated on producing the results which are presented in the following chapters.

Each of us would, of course, if we had the chance to write a book alone, have stressed different aspects. This book, however, is the outcome of a cooperative activity and also bears the marks of this in at least two aspects. Each of us had only a limited available space and was, therefore, severely handicapped with respect to the length and empirical strength of his or her argument. Moreover, we have insisted on having at least some chapters written by co-authors from different countries and this, of course, makes other kinds of compromises necessary. All in all, we have found our collaboration to be an intellectually and socially stimulating experience. Whether this form of cooperative comparative analysis is able to produce valuable results is up to our readers to decide.[6]

Notes

1. *Structural labilisation* refers to the process of the increasing detachment of traditional patterns of transition from school to work as manifested, for instance, in the relation between types of diplomas and types of jobs. It also refers to a clear increase in the difficulties and insecurities of a professional beginning and, connected with this, an increased professional and social risk for youth.

Marginalisation refers to the real and ideological process of assignment of economically and socially disadvantageous positions - such as unemployment or underemployment, for which the causes are ascribed to such groups themselves (Baethge *et al.*, 1980).

2. The project on Transition from School to Work forms part of the Vienna Centre's programme on Technology, Work and Society, in the various activities of which some 200 European social scientists are involved. Other activities of the Work Programme deal with:
- Conditions and Consequences of the Introduction of New Technology at Work;

- New Forms of Work Organisation;

- New Technologies and New Forms of Work Organisation;

- Wage and Payment Systems.

3. See appendix 1 for a list of the participating researchers.

4. See appendix 2.

5. Which does not imply that it is not praxis-oriented. Our aim has been mainly to develop a framework for understanding the phenomenon of Transition from School to Work in its present manifestations.

Such a framework provides the basis for a discussion about practical policy measures. This would, however, have to take into account the situation of specific groups of youth in specific national (or local) conditions. While we believe in the desirability of a general theoretical framework we do not believe in policy that is generally valid for 'the' European Youth.

6. We would like to express our sincere gratitude to all the institutes and institutions that have made it possible for us to meet: those who have kindly sponsored our workshops in Moscow, Sofia, Castelgandolfo, Barcelona, Lauf and Vienna as well as those who made our travels to and from these places possible.

2

Social Structure and Transition

Wladyslaw Adamski
and Katarzyna Staszynska

Introduction

This chapter is concerned with the process through which young people acquire social positions whereby there are at least two possibilities of understanding the term 'transition from school to work'. The first one is psychological in nature, the second one sociological. We have chosen the sociological interpretation of transition because we are more interested in the socio-structural determinants of this process of choice than in the psychological factors.

For our study, we have distinguished four groups of structural determinants

- demographic conditions;
- educational system and educational changes;
- changes in the social structure and mobility;
- demands in the labour market.

The most important factors of a sociological nature that influence the process of transition from school to work are twofold: first, while taking into account the needs and expectations of youth, demographic and educational trends and changes in the social structure; and second, industrialisation processes and the needs of the labour market.

In the first two sections of our paper we explain what the main structural factors of transition are in the countries under comparison. In the third section, we concentrate on the relationship between youth's expectations and actual labour market requirements. We assume that the educational systems play an important role in this field because schools not only mould youth's expectations but they also prepare young people for their occupational roles. We particularly emphasise the existing gap which exists between the expectations and aspirations of young people and the employment chances offered to them on the labour market. The most important consequences resulting from this situation are that young people tend to be either unemployed or underemployed, and underpaid. An additional consequence is their continuing economic dependence on their parents.

In the fourth section we describe these consequences and their effect on the social structure of society. Our special interest concerns the phenomenon of 'extended youth'. While this phenomenon can be found in both East and West European countries, we have observed a basic difference between the two due to the position of youth in society. In the East, the political policy of full employment contributes to low economic efficiency, while, in the West, unemployment has the effect of excluding from society those young people affected. Although this difference must not be neglected, there is also an important similarity: in both groups of countries, youth is steadily becoming a category of its own within the social structure. The question for further investigation is whether or not European youth can be considered to constitute a distinct social category with a 'quasi-class' character.

Demographic and Educational Expansion

What is common to most contemporary European societies is that, after the end of World War II, they witnessed a more or less spectacular rejuvenation of their populations. However, due to the uneven war losses, the effect of this 'baby boom' has varied in the different parts of Europe. Since the late 1950s, youth cohorts have become more clearly visible and 'felt' in Eastern than in Western countries. What really counts from the point of view of the possible chances and role of youth in society, is not only the absolute growth of the ascending young generation, but, above all, the ratio between the ascending 15-29 year-old age group and the stabilised 30-59 year-old one, and the variations in the magnitude of this ratio from one decade to another.

Table 2.1: Age cohorts of 15-39 as related to 30-59 years, as compared East and West European countries in the post-World War II decades

Country and years		Age cohorts (in thousands)		Ratio A/B	Change in ratio over preceding decade (%)
		A: 15-29	B: 30-59		
Bulgaria	1960	1 834	3 046	0 602	
	1970	1 922	3 355	0 574	- 4.7
	1981	1 905	2 937	0 648	+ 13.0
Czechoslovakia	1958	3 829	6 460	0 592	
	1968	2 796	5 270	0 530	- 10.5
	1979	3 470	4 963	0 699	+ 31.9
German Democratic Republic	1959	3 731	5 735	0 650	
	1969	4 512	7 671	0 588	- 9.6
	1981	4 062	6 216	0 653	+ 11.0
Hungary	1960	2 154	3 904	0 552	
	1970	2 437	3 948	0 617	+ 11.8
	1980	2 356	4 183	0 565	- 8.8
Poland	1960	6 442	10 510	0 612	
	1970	8 299	11 439	0 725	+ 18.5
	1980	9 475	12 972	0 730	+ 0.6
Romania	1956	4 684	5 483	0 854	
	1969	4 512	7 671	0 588	- 31.2
	1981	4 825	8 466	0 569	- 3.3
Yugoslavia	1958	5 010	5 603	0 894	
	1970	4 902	7 229	0 678	- 24.2
	1980	5 719	8 361	0 684	+ 0.8
France	1960	8 859	17 101	0 518	
	1970	11 336	17 606	0 643	+ 24.1
	1980	12 733	19 788	0 643	0.0
Germany, Federal Republic of	1960	12 282	21 257	0 578	
	1970	12 020	22 934	0 524	- 9.4
	1980	13 733	24 488	0 560	+ 6.9
The Netherlands	1960	2 490	3 851	0 695	
	1970	3 311	4 372	0 734	+ 5.6
	1980	3 554	5 048	0 705	- 4.0
Sweden	1960	1 993	3 050	0 653	
	1970	1 828	2 964	0 616	- 5.7
	1980	1 703	3 143	0 542	- 12.1
Great Britain and Northern Ireland	1960	10 763	18 911	0 569	
	1970	12 368	19 818	0 623	+ 9.5
	1980	12 640	20 469	0 617	- 1.0

Source: UN Demographic Yearbooks.

The data in Table 2.1 show us the following regularities:

- In the first post-war decade, up to the late 1950s, the highest proportion of youth in society occurred in Eastern Europe, specifically, in Romania and Yugoslavia. In the late 1950s, the young, ascending cohorts were almost equal in number to the older, stabilised ones.
- This picture changes substantially in the 1970s and 1980s. At this time the most impressive ratio of rejuvenation appears in Poland and the Netherlands.
- The lowest ratio of youth in the 1970s and 1980s is found in the Western part of Europe: in Sweden and the Federal Republic of Germany; in Eastern Europe, the lowest ratio is in Hungary and Romania. This may be taken as evidence that in those countries the pressure of demographic factors on both social structures and institutions is, at this time, relatively weak.
- As far as the ratio of the 1980s changes when compared with the 1970s, the highest increase is again found in Eastern Europe: in Czechoslovakia, followed by Bulgaria and the German Democratic Republic; while in the West, stagnant or decreasing tendencies prevail.
- When, however, we try to correlate both the rates of absolute growth of youth cohorts and their relative variations over time, then Poland shows the strongest cumulative and long-lasting effects of demographic rejuvenation.

It goes without saying that any sudden increase or fluctuation of youth cohorts unavoidably exerts heavy pressure on older generations and on a given society as well. It is quite obvious that this pressure challenges the educational system. How the countries of both Eastern and Western Europe have been successful in coping with the demographic highpoint is something we can judge on the basis of data included in Table 2.2.

To properly interpret the relevant statistics of educational development in both parts of Europe, it is necessary to take the different situations prevailing in each region after World War II into account:

- The countries of Eastern Europe had to pay incomparably higher costs than those in Western Europe to reconstruct their national economies, being more or less completely destroyed

by the war.
- In most cases, with the exception of Czechoslovakia and that part of pre-war Germany which became the German Democratic Republic, the East Europeans had to build up and modernise not only their educational systems but also backward or virtually non-existing industries, of which the latter had priority.

Table 2.2: Enrolment ratios for the third level of education, age cohorts 20-24 (%)

	1970	1975	1978	1979	1980	1981 male	1981 female	total
Eastern								
Bulgaria	14.4	19.2	17.7	16.6	15.7	13.8	16.8	15.3
Czechoslovakia	10.4	12.1	15.2	16.2	17.1	19.9	15.1	17.6
German Democratic Republic	32.8	29.4	29.1	30.4	30.4	24.8	36.3	30.4
Hungary	10.1	11.7	12.3	12.5	12.8	13.0	14.2	13.6
Poland	14.0	16.8	17.9	17.6	17.3	14.3	18.7	16.5
Romania	10.1	9.2	10.3	10.5	10.8	12.6	9.8	11.2
Yugoslavia	15.9	20.0	22.6	23.4	21.7	23.2[a]	20.1[a]	-
USSR	25.4	22.2	21.4	21.3	21.2	-	-	21.2
Western								
Austria	11.8	18.9	21.9	22.9	23.9	26.9	20.9	24.0
Finland	13.3	27.2	30.3	30.4	30.7	31.2[a]	30.1[a]	-
France	19.5	24.4	24.2	25.1	25.5	27.1[a]	23.9[a]	-
Germany, Federal Republic of	13.4	25.5	25.7	26.4	27.6	31.7[a]	23.3[a]	-
Italy	16.7	25.1	27.4	27.1	27.1	30.5[a]	23.6[a]	-
The Netherlands	19.5	25.5	28.6	30.1	30.5	35.9	26.1	31.1
Spain	8.9	20.4	22.4	23.2	23.2	25.7[a]	20.6[a]	-
Sweden	21.4	28.8	36.6	36.8	36.9	38.3	35.4	36.8

[a]Data from 1980.

Source: *UNESCO Statistical Yearbook*, 1983.

What has been achieved in Eastern Europe under these circumstances in the post-war period might justly be called an educational revolution.

When trying to compare the ratios of East and West European student enrolment at the third level of educational institutions (see Table 2.2), it is important to keep in mind not only the relative weight of youth cohorts in demographic structures, as indicated in Table 2.1, but also the levels of economic development.

Except for Sweden, which is so far ahead in this aspect that comparisons are impossible, West European countries show, on the average, slightly higher ratios of enrolment at the third level of education than is the case in Eastern Europe. At the same time, it should not be overlooked that in this aspect the German Democratic Republic, Yugoslavia and the Soviet Union are almost equal to, and in some instances are better than, some Western countries. Also speaking in favour of Eastern countries are the educational opportunities offered to women. With the exception of Yugoslavia, Romania and Czechoslovakia, these chances are equal to or even higher than those offered to men, while in Western Europe, except for the Scandinavian countries, the educational systems remain highly unfavourable to women.

In addition to demographic and economic factors, ideological justifications and political requirements should also be carefully considered when looking for and trying to explain why the educational policies in Eastern Europe have been so concerned with the equalizing functions of the school system. In order to rebuild the ranks of the intelligentsia and link this stratum with the goals set forth by the social revolution, a system of privileges was established for young people stemming from worker and peasant families. Special selective procedures for these applicants were introduced and, what appears to have been most instrumental in this respect is a special, fairly developed system of evening and extramural (non-resident) schooling on every level of post-elementary education for all young employees willing to complete or continue education.

The expansion of special schooling for blue-collar workers in Eastern Europe has been quite impressive. On the eve of the 1980s, the share of extramural students remained at the same level as it had been two decades earlier, with the highest levels being reached in Hungary and Poland. In these two countries, this type of student constituted more than one third of the total number of students continuing their education, while in the German Democratic Republic and Romania this class of students drastically dropped to the level of one-fifth of the student population in the 1980s. Despite this more recent tendency, there is no doubt that the extended system of extramural studies, which has been extremely popular in socialist countries for many years, has substantially added to the overall education of the young generation. This is especially true if we consider the system of education as a vehicle for intragenerational mobility.

The expansion of education should also be discussed as an important factor contributing to the intergenerational gap. The differences in the average educational level among younger and older generations in all countries are obvious. However, this gap in education between two generations is much stronger in Eastern countries than in the West. For example, in Austria and in Poland, the proportion of men having only an elementary education decreased sharply in the early 1950s, and this diminishing tendency remained in both countries.[1] However, it is important to notice that these proportions were, from the very beginning, much lower in Austria in every age cohort than in Poland. Similarly, the proportion of persons with secondary schooling or higher levels of education is higher in every age cohort in Austria than in the respective cohorts of Polish job beginners. The comparison of educational structures of the groups beginning their first job in both countries makes between the periods 1945-1949 and 1970-1971 clearly visible that the educational structure offered to Polish youth in the 1970s was very much like that offered Austrian job beginners in the late 1940s.[2] The intergenerational gap with respect to achievements in education still remains stronger in the less industrialised Eastern countries than in the more industrialised Eastern countries.

In addition, the number of students at the third level of education increased noticeably in West European countries starting in 1970. In the same period, this growth was somewhat slower in the Eastern countries. However, the relative weights of this growth must be considered differently in different groups of countries. The stable growth of student population in Eastern countries needs to be considered in light of the phase of development that followed the stage of rapid industrialisation. Relatively similar, although weaker, tendencies were observed in the less-industrialised Western countries such as Italy, where the growth of the student population in the 1970s was only slightly lower than it was in Austria or Sweden.

According to Treiman's (1970) hypothesis, one explanation for these phenomena is that they are influenced by the present stage of industrial development.[3] The rapid changes in social structure and the expansion in education are connected to the rapid changes in national economies (e.g. as was the case in Eastern countries in the period between 1945 and the early 1970s). After a period of economic expansion, changes in social structure tend to reach rather stable levels (e.g. well-industrialised Western countries in the post-war period). The next significant stage in the transformation of the social structure comes with the next period of economic development: that of the expansion of new technologies (e.g. well-industrialised Western countries from the 1970s to the present). Treiman's hypothesis allows us to explain why the education gap between given generations is much stronger in Eastern countries than in Western ones, and also why it is slightly stronger in less-industrialised than in well-industrialised Western countries.

In summarising, we can stress three common features of European societies:

-   a demographic expansion of youth cohorts is more or less visible in both parts of Europe;
-   there is an increasing level of average education in the younger generations (not only as compared to older generations, but also when taking the older and younger sections of the cohorts of the young generation into account;
-   there is an education gap between generations (which is larger in the less-industrialised societies).

Mobility trends: social openness versus closeness

As was said before, the educational expansion and the intergenerational gap in the educational levels resulting from it may be explained using Treiman's hypothesis on the impact of economic development on transformations of social structure as a basis.

This hypothesis, however, is formulated on the level of a global society where individual paths of mobility do not play an important role. Thus, he is actually dealing on the macro-social level with the effect of a huge number of these individual paths of mobility. However, it must be stressed that the degree of openness of mobility channels is what determines these individual paths of mobility and the mobility chances of individuals. In other words, mobility trends,when observed at the level of a global society, are what determine the shape of individual life paths. Thus, the transition from school to work should be analysed as an effect of a structure of social mobility. The changes in the mobility patterns in different countries can be treated as an important factor determining the conditions of transition from school to work by young people.

Treiman's hypothesis says, above all, that the process of industrialisation results in transformations in social structure which, in turn, result from a high degree of structural mobility (this is because the structure of the labour market and the number of posts are permanently under modification which, in turn, reduces the influence of the inheritance mechanism on mobility). Consequently, in more industrialised societies, the direct influence of educational achievements on processes of social mobility increases, and the educational systems, being more open, become direct mobility channels. However, after completing the phase of expansive industrialisation, social mobility stabilises at a more or less permanent level until a subsequent phase of intensive economic transformation is reached.

This hypothesis enables us to distinguish three groups of countries in terms of their level of openness of social structure (or of high mobility) associated with the level of industrialisation. The first group is composed of highly developed Western countries (for example Sweden and the Federal Republic of Germany) which have entered a new phase of industrialisation by means of expansion of new technologies which, once again, have modified the labour market structure. In the period between 1945 and the early 1970s, these countries have moved from a phase of relative stabilisation of social mobility to once of increased mobility.

The second group of countries is composed of less-industrialised Western countries, such as Italy and Spain, where the phase of intensive industrialisation has not been fully completed and where social mobility has remained at a relatively high level. The third group consists of the East European countries, where the period of intensive industrialisation has already been completed together with a period of intensive social mobility (i.e. of mobility forced by structural transformations). These countries will move next from a phase of open social structure to one of relative stabilisation of mobility processes.

However, classification of the countries in question into three groups based on the character of mobility processes, using Treiman's hypothesis as a guide, is inappropriate given the available data. First, two East European countries are on the extreme ends of the scale as far as the level of openness of social structure is concerned - it is high in Hungary and relatively low in Poland.[4] It seems that differentiation among patterns of social mobility in socialist countries may be a consequence not only of the levels of industrialisation but also of some additional factors as well, in particular, of the extent to which agriculture has been collectivised.[5] Second, two types of countries may be specified within the highly industrialised Western countries: one type enjoys relatively high mobility (such as the Netherlands and Sweden); the other type has a relatively low mobility (such as the Federal Republic of Germany and France).[6] The differentiation in patterns of mobility in the highly industrialised Western countries may be explained by the influence the openness of educational structures has on its working force. The independence of educational achievements from the social origin is considerably higher in Sweden and in the Netherlands than in the Federal Republic of Germany or in France. Similarly, one cannot exclude the influence of social policy on patterns of mobility and on the shape of educational systems. However, it is worth emphasizing that in all these countries there has been a tendency to close some of the privileged socio-vocational categories such as large-scale ownership and the scholarly professions.[7]

A relatively low level of openness of chances existed in two countries with a low level of industrialisation - in Italy and Spain. This result was certainly heavily influenced by the structure of the school systems in both countries and by the traditionally strong social differentiation which exists (in Spain 5% of the population with the highest incomes receives some 20% of the total income). This factor has to be taken into consideration when explaining differentiation in patterns of mobility in countries with similar levels of economic development (for instance, in the Federal Republic of Germany, the concentration of incomes in the upper 5% of the population is more than 30% of the total income earned by the entire population).[8] In other words, the existing social differentiation is decisive for estimating the extent to which the growth of industrialisation affects transformations in social structure.[9] In general, we can therefore conclude that patterns of social mobility and levels of openness of social structure depend on something more than just the level of economic development of a country.

Comparative data on social mobility were mostly gathered in

the early 1970s. Thus, in order to answer the question, under what circumstances is vocational initiation of youth taking place nowadays, we need to determine what kind of changes in mobility tendencies have taken place in the 1970s and the 1980s. To illustrate these tendencies, we will use Poland and France as examples.

Poland is a good example for the statement that in the Eastern countries social structure would become increasingly closed once the phase of construction of the economy and of the social system were completed. Indeed, from studies on social mobility, a tendency is shown for mobility to decrease both in intra- and intergenerational dimensions, as is particularly clearly demonstrated in the 1970s and the early 1980s.[10]

A similar tendency is also observed in France, which has moved from the group of countries of relatively high social mobility in the 1980s to one of insignificant mobility in the 1980s. One may say that dissimilarities in the patterns of social mobility (systemic 'built-in' social inequalities in Western societies and an increase in such inequalities in Eastern countries after completion of the phase of structural transformation) do not allow for the same explanation of this common tendency.[11] Yet, it is worth stressing that each European society is an isolated social system, insensible to the situation prevailing in the world economy. For this reason, the Treiman's hypothesis cannot automatically be used for the purpose of forecasting the extent of social mobility on the basis of the pace of industrialisation. Thus, surprisingly, a decrease in social mobility in France may be explained by the situation in the world economy in the 1970s, i.e. by the economic crisis which has affected more or less all the countries of Western Europe. Consequently, the example of France may be representative for most of the industrialised European countries if it is assumed that the particular rules of the social policies practiced in some countries (for instance, in Sweden or in the Netherlands) did not level the impact of pure economic factors on the tendencies of transformations of social structure.

In conclusion, we want to state that despite a lack of the latest data on the scale of social mobility in most of the countries under examination, expectations about the openness of their social structures do not seem to be realised under the circumstances prevalent in the 1970s and 1980s. This is partially caused by factors of structural character (such as the completion of the phase of intensive transformations in the Eastern countries) and partially

- by factors of purely economic character (such as the economic crisis in Western Europe). Also significant is the extent of people's social expectations from mobility processes (any blocking of mobility under the circumstances of relative openness of social structure becomes, from the point of view of the public, a symptom of radical diminution in mobility and is seen as a closing of channels for social improvement). We suppose, therefore, that in most of the countries under examination a relative limitation of dislocation possibilities within the given social structure has taken place both subjectively and objectively in the 1970s and 1980s. Thus, young people have found themselves in a situation where their expectations concerning the role played by the education system in mobility processes (and so concerning the role of individual achievement in the process of locating social position) turned out not to be realised.

Labour market requirements and youth's expectations

In the Eastern countries, regulations of an institutional nature tend to bring youth's aspirations in line with labour market requirements and to overcome (in accordance with the ideology of equal opportunity) the traditional recruiting mechanisms to social positions.[12] These institutional or legislative regulations are based on the assumption that the educational system, as managed and controlled by the state, is able to adapt the form of youth's aspirations, and their professional preparation, to the requirements of the national economy and to the needs of the labour market while offering at the same time - irrespective of social background but in accordance with individual capabilities - relatively equal chances to everybody. It is assumed, therefore, that the educational system plays the role of the main mechanism of social mobility.

The last two decades have, however, revealed some clearly visible disturbances in the operation and efficiency of the educational systems in the Eastern countries. These disturbances resulted, in almost all countries, in perceptible divergences between the aspirations of youth entering the labour market and the needs of the labour market.[13] These divergences manifest themselves either in a relatively high level of professional fluctuations within a short time after transition from school to work, or in frequent supplementary education during employment

41

in order to adjust the qualifications possessed to the labour market possibilities.[14]

Both phenomena may also be treated as a result of individual behaviour which is aiming at adjusting one's own professional aspirations to the possibilities for satisfying them. Such an interpretation is confirmed, for example, in changes in youth's educational decisions that have become noticeable lately in Poland as well as in the Soviet Union. In both countries, a tendency can be observed that young people are less inclined to choose general secondary schooling and the classical type of university education. This can be seen as an indication of youth's increased realism in evaluating the possibilities that the labour market and the national economy provide them.[15]

On the basis of the data available, one may also question the assumption concerning the openness of the social structure and the existence of equal opportunity irrespective of social background. In at least two East European countries, traditional mechanisms of selection to social positions and a tendency to inherit social status seem to be of significant importance: in Hungary and Poland. In Hungary, where social mobility was higher than in Poland but where, since the early 1970s, social mobility has visibly diminished, the influence of the social status of parents on the educational and professional positions reached by their children is not as extensive as it is in Poland.[16] However, the Hungarian figures clearly manifest the existence of traditional mechanisms of selection to social positions. It also appears that the requirements of the educational institutions go beyond the abilities of a substantial number of students; some 20% of all Hungarian students do not complete primary education within the expected eight years.[17]

An important example of youth's situation on the labour market is - on a different scale in different countries - a misadaptation of the young generation's capabilities when it comes to fulfilling socio-professional roles. In Poland this is, for instance, expressed in the relatively low participation of youth in political, trade unionist and innovative activities. Similar phenomena are observed in other countries.[18] In addition, a tendency observed in Poland to look for a job outside the state sector - in Polonia's firms or in private enterprises - proves that at least a part of younger staff is misadapted to the socioprofessional roles offered to them by the national economy. In the light of the above observations the regulating role of the educational systems in some of the Eastern countries seems to be an ideal rather than an accomplished standard.

The existing differences between the school systems in the Eastern and Western countries do not allow for full comparability of these systems as social mobility institutions. The role of educational institutions in processes of social mobility is, however, worth looking at in analysing their role in global societies.

A number of cases observed in the West European countries give evidence for the fact that disfunctions in the regulating role of the school systems are, next to the economic and technological changes in the 1970s and the 1980s, one of the main causes for the problems in youth's transition from school to work.

In many Western countries it also happens that young people are employed outside their acquired professions.[19] In Austria, for example, some 50 per cent of the employed youth is concerned. In Italy and the Netherlands the present labour market situation not only leads to younger generations having to choose jobs which are inconsistent with their qualifications, but also to frequent changes of work, or even profession, within the initial years of employment after the transition from school to work. Thus, it appears that the educational systems in these countries are subject to slower changes than the technological and economic situation on the labour market calls for.

A phenomenon which is connected with the divergence between the qualifications possessed and the job carried out is a process of making young people's aspirations more realistic by way of initial job experiences.[20] The frequent cases of short-term, on-the-job education, may be considered to be indicators of this process. The attempt to make aspirations more realistic basically boils down to limiting or renouncing them. As a result of this type of experience gathered on the labour market self-interest in work is being replaced in the set of work values by job security.[21] Italian studies have pointed at the phenomenon that young people tend to accept almost any job, even irrespective of its quality and conformity with their aspirations and qualifications.[22]

But a more serious consequence of the gap between youth's professional expectations and what the labour markets have to offer in the Western countries is unemployment. Youth between the ages of 15 and 25 are among those groups of professionally active people who are the most strongly represented among the unemployed. To mention only two examples: in Italy, the national unemployment rate was 9.9% in 1983, in the 1980s, the unemployment rate in the 14-19 year-old age group has reached 30%, and for the 20-29 year-olds, it is as high as 46.5%;[23] in Finland, the national unemployment rate was equal to 6.1% in 1983, but in 1980 for those between the ages of 15-19, it has reached 17%, and for those between the ages of 20-24, it is 10%. At the same time, it has diminished to 5.5%, which is even below the national average, for those in the 25-29 year-old age bracket.[24] This means that the young who are looking for their first job are among the most affected by unemployment and that the unemployment level in the youngest age group determines, to a large extent, the national average.

The shortage of jobs in Western countries has resulted in increased competition among the employed. The gap between the school qualifications of young people and labour market needs has resulted in a situation in which people who are already gainfully employed and professionally experienced (and thus, by definition, belong to the older age groups) appear to be privileged irrespective of their educational level. At the very moment the younger generation enters the competition of the labour market, the chances of its members gaining employment is much lower than that of older generations who have already been employed, in spite of the higher level of qualifications which the younger generation offers. The older generations are not only privileged by the existing mechanisms and criteria of the labour market, but are also placed in a position of blocking the chances of younger generations.[25] Such competition, favouring older and more professionally experienced individuals, occurs also, in a number of socialist countries where - except for Yugoslavia - unemployment does not exist.[26] Intergenerational competition in the Eastern countries does not play a very important role when one is looking for just any kind of employment, but it does do so when the problem is to get a better job - that is to say, one which is better paid and more in line with the applicant's education and qualifications. As a result, just as some young people in Western countries find employment outside the official labour market, so, too, do young people in Eastern countries.

It appears, however, that such consequences, resulting from the gap between the labour market and the school system that we described earlier, are not of the same concern to all youth in the West. In Italy, for instance, those groups particularly threatened during the transition from school to work are the children with a lower- and middle-class background, who live in less-industrialised regions where the education is traditional.[27] Similar criteria lead to distinguishing a category of 'discriminated' groups (with respect to the chances of getting a job or getting a job congruent with one's aspirations) in Spain, where interregional differences and social background play an even more essential role than in Italy.[28] Moreover, also in the Western countries, social class still influences young people's educational chances.[29]

The distinct features of youth's social status in the West European countries may be described in the following way:

- a high risk of unemployment directly after completing one's education;
- low chances for changing one's professional situation through additional training, i.e. low intragenerational mobility;
- a strong tendency to inherit the social status of the parents (diminishing intergenerational mobility); and
- the deprivation of one's aspirations in life.[30]

The synthetic characteristic of youth's social situation in the East European countries may be described as follows:

- a high level of deprivation of life and professional aspirations just aft.r the transition from school to work;
- an increasing tendency to inherit parental social status (diminishing intergenerational mobility); and
- a high risk of underemployment and underpayment in the initial period of professional activity.

A common feature of youth's social situation in both groups of countries is the strong deprivation of life aspirations and the lack of economic independence long after one's education has been completed.

Extended youth and the revolution
of rising aspirations

It is common knowledge that in present-day Europe, as observed from the generational perspective, the scope of youth tends to rapidly expand in terms of both age and social status. As far as age is concerned, this expansion applies mostly to the upper limits of youth cohorts. Contrary to the logic of well-established definitions, the line which divides youth from adulthood is moving upwards, far beyond the boundary of those 24-25 year-olds and more often including as youth those who are approaching 30 or even 35.[31] From the point of view of social structure, this means that the category of youth, besides encompassing pupils and students, will gradually embrace a majority of young people who are gainfully employed but who, in spite of this, for many years remain far from achieving the status of economic and social independence which is typical of full adulthood. One of the consequences of this process is that youth researchers and politicians will have a growing interest in those who are looking for employment or who have just entered the job market, rather than in dropouts and students.

In trying to define the process of transition from school to work, it is quite easy to establish when it starts, but it is not clear at what point it has taken place. The approach which seems to prevail in most of the Western societies, openly or implicitly, is that when the school-leaver gets a job, particularly if it is a permanent one, this marks the end of the transition process. This assumption, however, does not fully apply to all societies in Europe, and especially not in the Eastern countries.

Any serious attempt to integrate within society the young people of today who are entering the stage of extended youth has to go beyond the employment - unemployment axis, and to the very roots of the phenomenon. The increasing problems that we can observe in the transition from school to work should indeed be considered as the reflection of a crisis; but the much broader process of transition from youth to adulthood, of which this is a part, does not just concern narrowly defined educational institutions and the labour market. Based on our data, we can show how this transition period tends to develop in two directions simultaneously:

- the transition embraces a broader *social space*, and is rooted not only in the family, the school and work organisations, but also in some intermediary 'institutions' such as part-time employment, forced or voluntary unemployment, under-employment, deferred entry into the labour force through continued schooling, and so on; and
- the transition takes a *longer time* which, in order to be dealt with, tends increasingly to require political intervention by the government.

The post World War II development of European countries shows certain striking similarities, in spite of their cultural and systemic peculiarities. In our view, the most important of them has been the vast scale of increased social aspirations. Striving for better education, higher socio-vocational status, and higher standards of material and cultural consumption has become a mass phenomenon characteristic of all the social classes. This revolution of rising expectations also took place in the consciousness and behaviour of the younger generations, and especially in the 'baby-boom generations' whose life orientations were being shaped in the long period of uninterrupted economic expansion.

The 1960s, and in some countries, the early 1970s, seemed to confirm the optimistic vision that those growing aspirations could be satisfied. The explosive growth of schools, incessant increases in the number of new jobs, and increased social mobility offered if not a guarantee, then at least chances for a rapid fulfillment of ambitious targets in life careers. This situation has changed, however. The present trend of economic development is not only bringing a general slowdown or even a drastic disruption of growth, but is making the possibility of a quick return to a period of expansion unlikely. One of the important consequences of these tendencies will be a further deterioration and complication of the conditions which determine the transition processes and careers of the younger generations, and, consequently, an expansion of the extended youth category.

These trends make us look at the 1980s as a separate period of social development in all countries of Europe, irrespective of their systemic affiliations. The period of the 1970s and 1980s has been marked, on the one hand, by an unabating, and in some instances still growing, supply of high aspirations and sociovocational needs and, on the other hand, by clearly reduced or selective opportunities for satisfying them. Those limitations will be felt not only in the sphere of incomes and material consumption or in attempts to get access to higher positions in sociovocational structures, but also in a growing interest to take part in the very decision-making that might affect the future of workers and citizens. It seems that for both Eastern and Western systems, their further development will depend to a higher degree than it has in the past on the outcome of the clash between, and the confrontation with, unsatisfied expectations and existing socioeconomic and political structures.

In both parts of Europe, the origins of this intergenerational growth of aspirations is to be found in the main trend of post-war socioeconomic changes. They were marked by the ideology of 'equal chances' and 'social justice'. But, contrary to what is claimed by representatives of technological and economic determinism, we do not think that aspirations - manifested in needs, value systems and dominant life orientations - can be examined only as products of structural changes. One has to assume, instead, that social aspirations, viewed from the historical perspective of the 1980s, deserve to be treated as a more or less autonomous phenomenon and capable of affecting the trends of fundamental changes within societies.

In both West and East European countries the investments young people make to acquire school qualifications is not compensated for by adequate socio-professional positions. At least, in some socialist countries, individuals that have 'invested' in education and have acquired a university degree, and sometimes even secondary school-leavers, are unable to find an appropriate job. One of the most harmful results of this is a high level of labour turnover which especially occurs in the initial years after the transition from school to work. Another consequence is a decreasing interest to study in secondary comprehensive schools and universities. There is also evidence that, on the labour market, the older generation blocks the chances for the younger one. This is quite clearly visible when their access to more qualified and responsible positions is analysed.

In the Western countries the results of competition on the labour market prove that very often professional experience and a 'long-residence' period at a job are more required than formal school qualifications. School credentials are no longer sufficient to get a job that would match youth's qualifications and aspirations and, moreover, it is often not sufficient to get any gainful employment at all. Thus, the young generation is significantly more deprived of work than the older one and is forced to change professions and to acquire still further qualifications.

The ideology of social advancement and of openness of social structure appeared to be, in the face of the above-mentioned structural hinderances, quite different from the social experiences of the young generations. There is no doubt that our societies will have to pay for any deprivation being sustained by young generations at the time of their transition from school to work. In the Eastern countries the full-employment policies protect youth against one of the most serious forms of deprivation, namely unemployment, but the unexpected result of this is that the young are quite often employed irrespective of their qualifications and aspirations and are also paid below the reasonably determined social minimum. Under these circumstances, the responsibility for satisfying the needs of the young generations is being transferred to their parents, and this, in addition, again extends the period of youth in an artificial way. On the other hand, the economic systems of the Eastern countries pay for sticking to the policies of full employment - one of the most severe results of this is low economic efficiency. The reverse trend in the Western countries produces another type of deprivation among youth trying to get into the labour market. As a consequence, a heavy financial burden resulting from youth unemployment is being born by state institutions and trade unions.

The extension of the stage of youth in both systems becomes a source of the most serious deprivation of the young generations, i.e. deprivation of aspirations in relation to their contribution in the distribution of social and material goods. The phenomenon is particularly severe in the Eastern countries where the pool of goods available for social distribution has not been as abundant as elsewhere. The lack of economic independence for youth, due to unemployment in the West and to underemployment and/or underpayment caused by the policy of full employment in the East, has become the main factor responsible for youth becoming a separate category within the social structure. This allows us to hypothesise that the young generations of contemporary Europe tend to form a distinct category of a quasi-social class character.

Notes

1. See M. Haller and B.W. Mach, 'Structural Changes and Mobility in a Capitalist and a Socialist Society; A Comparison of Men in Austria and Poland' in M. Niessen, J. Peschar and Ch. Kourilsky (eds), *International Comparative Research. Social Structures and Public Institutions in Eastern and Western Europe* (Pergamon Press, Oxford, 1984), pp. 43-103.

2. Haller and Mach, ibid., Table 2.

3. See D.J. Treiman, 'Industrialisation and Social Stratification' in E.O. Laumann (ed.), *Social Stratification*, (Bobbs-Merrill, Indianapolis-New York, 1970), pp. 207-34.

4. See A. Tyree, M. Semyonov and R.W. Hodge, Table 2. 'Gaps and Glissandos: Inequalities, and Social Mobility in 24 Countries',

American Sociological Review, vol. 44, 1979, pp. 410-22.

5. See Z. Sawinski and H. Domanski, *Wymiary struktury spolecznej. Analiza porównawcza* (Dimension of Social Structure. A Comparative Analysis), (Ossolineum, Warsaw, 1986).

6. Sawinski and Domanski, ibid., chapter 4.

7. Sawinski and Domanski, ibid.

8. Tyree, Semyonov and Hodge, 'Gaps and Glissandos', Table 2.

9. Tyree, Semyonov and Hodge, ibid., pp. 417-18.

10. See I. Bialecki, *Zmiany ruchliwosci spolecznej*, forthcoming.

11. Haller and Mach, 'Structural Changes'.

12. See T. Babushkina and V. Shubkin, 'On the Problem of Transition from School to Work', 1984; M. Stefanov, 'The Transition from School to Work (An Attempt at a Sociological Approach to the Problem)', 1984.

13. Babushkina and Shubkin, ibid.; A. Hoffman, 'Aspects of the Transition from School to Work in the German Democratic Republic', 1984; P. Molnar, 'School Career and the First Job', 1984.

14. On-the-job education is an integral part of the educational systems in the socialist countries.

15. Systematic figures on this topic are not available in Poland; for the Soviet Union the figures cover the Novosibirsk region, thus they do not create a sufficient basis for any generalisation.

16. Molnar, 'School Career'; K. Worotynska, 'Transition from School to Work, Poland 1973-1984', 1984.

17. Molnar, ibid., Tables 14 and 15.

18. In regard to the German Democratic Republic, it is stated: 'In spite of many advances, the majority of young people still shows too little interest in innovational activities, and they are not strongly enough oriented toward their own activity and the solving of their occupational problems' (Hoffman, 'Aspects of the Transition'); in relation to Bulgaria: 'At times indifference to work is to be observed in young people, and sometimes even deviation from the work process'. (Stefanov, 'The Transition from School to Work').

19. L. Battistoni, 'New Technologies, Youth Employment and Transition from School to Work', 1984; B. Hövels, 'Recent Dutch Studies on the Transition from School to Work', 1984; I. Knapp, 'New Technologies, Youth Employment and Transition from School to Work', 1984.

20. Hövels, ibid.; M.V. Volanen, 'How Does a Young Adult Settle Down in a Vocation?', 1984.

21. Battistoni, 'New Technologies'.

22. Battistoni, ibid.

23. *Year Book of Labour Statistics 1984*, ILO; Battistoni, ibid., Table 8.

24. *Year Book of Labour Statistics 1984*, ILO; Volanen, 'How does a Young Adult Settle Down', Table 8.

25. J. Hartmann, 'Transition from School to Work in Sweden', 1985; Hövels, 'Recent Dutch Studies'; Knapp, 'New Technologies, Youth Employment and Transition from School to Work'.

26. S. Drobnic, 'Transition from School to Work in Yugoslavia', 1984.

27. Battistoni, 'New Technologies'.

28. J. Casal, M. Ludevid, M. Medio and J. Planas, 'The Transition from School to Work in Spain', 1984.

29. Casal, Ludevid, Medio, Planas, ibid.; Hövels, 'Recent Dutch Studies'.

30. See Knapp, 'New Technologies, Youth Employment and Transition from School to Work'.

31. J.S. Coleman, *Youth: Transition to Adulthood*, (Washington D.C., 1974).

3

Professional Aspirations and Society's Needs

Vladimir Shubkin, Yuri Emeljanov

Introduction

The dynamic process of transition from school to work develops under the simultaneous, and sometimes contradictory, impact of different factors. Despite similarities in the general composition of these factors which influence the process of transition, there are also substantial differences in both the character and the impact of those factors within the different European countries. Hence, the task of comparing the results achieved by national studies about the problems of transition is both worthy and challenging.

This chapter presents an attempt to make a comparison based on an analytical framework developed in the Soviet Union more than twenty years ago.[1] This framework is first presented and subsequently applied to an analysis of transition problems in Eastern and Western Europe. The empirical data are taken from the national reports prepared during our joint project.

The Structural Conflict During the Transition from School to Work

Our earlier research showed the strong influence of different factors on the transition from school to work. These included the country's stage of economic development and the ensuing requirements in manpower; demographic trends and the quantitative impact of young generations; structures of, and developments in, the educational system; and the dynamics of young people's personal aspirations. At the same time, research demonstrated that the development of all these factors is far from simultaneous. Economic growth follows its own regularities and so do demographic trends. The system of education, too, develops according to given principles, and these are considerably removed from both the requirements of society and the aspirations of youth. A further factor is that the aspirations and expectations of young people develop, to a certain extent, independently.

It is an incredibly complex task to unite all these developments and to provide for their planned and proportionate development. In addition, the contradictory character of the development of social subsystems increases under the conditions of the modern scientific-technical revolution. A tendency emerges towards their respective autonomisation, which is difficult to overcome.[2] As a result, inevitable contradictions turn up

- between the requirements of the labour market and the growth (or reduction) of the employable population;
- between the requirements of the economy for certain specialists and the educational system which ignores these demands;
- between the needs of the economy for manpower with specific vocational training and the professional aspirations of youth.

Figure 3.1: Professional aspirations of youth and the manpower requirements of society (by professions)

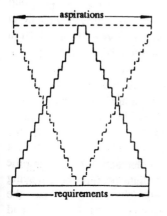
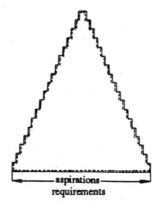

Simultaneously, a certain interference between social subsystem processes also takes place - with the result that imbalances acquire distorted proportions and, from time to time, become acute. In many European countries today, this can be seen quite clearly in the contradiction between the manpower requirements of society (by professions) and the professional aspirations of youth. It is this contradiction which cannot be ignored while analysing the processes of transition from school to work.

The relation between these two structures may be illustrated by a simple model (see Figure 3.1).

Suppose a certain society has a number of professions, and we know: 1) how many workers of each profession society requires; 2) the prestige and attractiveness of each profession among young people who are looking to begin employment and 3) how many of them are going to work in, or study for, a given profession.

Let us place professions by their attractiveness in such a way that the most desired professions are put at the top of the list; and let us mark the need in manpower on the horizontal axis.

Let us assume that need for manpower is greatest in the least attractive professions and lowest in the more attractive professions. As a result, we shall get something like the pyramid drawn by a dense line.

Now let us imagine that we have questioned the young adults who are going to fill the jobs, university halls, and vocational and technical schools which are marked by the dense-line pyramid. Many studies show that, as a rule, young people strive for the most attractive professions, where the need for workers is usually not big.[3] At the base of the pyramid, the situation is reversed: there are by far more vacancies than applicants. If we mark the number of young adults who would like to have jobs in a given profession, then we would get a second (dotted) pyramid, which would be a mirror-like reflection of the first one. Thus, the vacancies indicated by the dense-line pyramid would be confronted with the aspirations of the dotted-line pyramid.

If we now were to add the third element - the educational system - it would occupy an intermediate position between the structure of a society's requirements for manpower and the professional aspirations of its young people.

Requirements applicants must fulfill - a school diploma, university diploma, and/or other necessary qualifications - are most demanding at the top of the pyramid, where the most

54

attractive occupations are placed; and are generally less demanding at the bottom of the pyramid, where the need for applicants is greater than the supply of job seekers. The educational system and its separate links may be directed either at the structure of vacancies, or at the professional inclinations of youth.

The structure of a society's manpower requirements - that is, the structure of vacancies which a society provides for young people through the labour market or through the employment system - is conditioned by the interaction of a number of factors, including the peculiarities of the existing socio-economic regime, technology, the social division of labour, historical and cultural traditions, and so on. Evidently, this structure is only subject to change over the long run. The structure of aspirations depends, to a great extent, on the evaluation young people make of professions. It is clear that this structure is more flexible and changeable than the first one.

A comparison of job evaluations made by secondary school leavers in Novosibirsk in the 1980s with the evaluations made by those who graduated twenty years ago permits one to see the dynamics of the prestige given to professions.

The past twenty years are characterised by a growth of realism among young people. It appears that a certain increase in maturity has taken place among seventeen year-olds. More so than before, real social needs have been taken into account. Consequently, an obvious decline in the prestige of scientific professions has taken place. While jobs in agriculture and in the service sector were once judged to be the least prestigious kinds of work, this attitude has changed considerably. These trends are typical for both young men and women in Novosibirsk. It is the case, however, that girls estimated the prestige of intellectual jobs such as high school teacher, physician, and biologist much higher than boys did.

If we make a similar comparison in rural areas, these trends can be seen even more clearly.[4] (See Table 3.1)

The scale of prestige associated with professions is a rather delicate instrument which makes it possible to detect changes in people's consciousness. As a result, in the Soviet Union, it was found that the changes along this scale do reflect broader changes in social life, in particular, changes in the social composition of secondary school graduates after the introduction of universal secondary school education. It is obvious that prestige ratings are also very much conditioned by the wider societal context and, therefore, profound international differences may occur. We have been able to trace such differences in a comparative research project undertaken in the socialist countries of Europe; one example from three of these countries may suffice to indicate the impact of national traditions and situations.

Table 3.1: Changes of estimates in the prestige accorded to professions for 20 years (1983 to 1963) (%)

Professions	Novosibirsk		Novosibirsk rural area	
	Young men	Young women	Young men	Young women
Vendor	152.97	175.57	176.211	181.05
Animal tender	146.47	132.58	120.31	103.22
Driver	137.45	112.55	144.52	09.07
Tractor driver	125.94	103.05	106.28	102.92
Waiter	123.14	104.90	110.70	118.13
Accountant	116.20	135.74	118.66	160.87
Machinist	101.76	96.58	128.68	100.56
Biologist (scientist)	90.31	104.38	89.38	110.41
Physician	89.87	103.43	96.43	105.73
Teacher of history	89.58	100.00	93.94	104.87
High school teacher	84.38	102.32	84.17	100.41
Bricklayer	95.31	106.13	97.78	95.08
Textile worker	97.95	89.08	95.31	94.03
Fitter	97.76	95.29	86.15	80.30
Engineer	77.16	71.75	82.48	75.09
Physicist (scientist)	74.17	79.04	71.33	91.80
Assembly worker in construction	70.65	80.00	87.46	72.50

While in all countries both unskilled and highly skilled workers gave intellectual professions the highest marks and manual work and work in services low marks, there are differences reflecting national peculiarities. Bulgarian workers gave the writing profession, which is very popular in Hungary and the Soviet Union, the lowest marks. Hungarian youth considers being a waiter, which is very unpopular among the young people of Bulgaria and the Soviet Union, to be prestigious. Soviet youth considers being a metallurgist to be of high prestige, but this is one of the least desirable professions among the youth of Bulgaria.

Surely the development of international economic cooperation may narrow some of the differences found in these judgments, but one can hardly expect the judgments to disappear completely within the coming decades as they are connected to the development of production forces and historical and cultural traditions.

The contradiction between aspirations and society's requirements when demand is higher than supply

So far, we have considered the contradiction between society's manpower requirements and the vocational aspirations of youth assuming that there is a balance between society's requirements and the number of job seekers on the labour market. In fact, such is a very particular case, and quite often these two structures are not balanced at all. We have either a shortage of manpower - which occurs when the economy's requirements are not covered by the number of youth entering the work force - or unemployment, which occurs when there is a lower demand for the skills being offered by the labour force (including youth).

In the socialist countries, the employment situation is characterised by a certain contradiction between aspirations and requirements and - in a number of cases - a demand which is higher than the supply. This situation is aggravated by a demographic decline.

The contradiction between a society's manpower requirements and youth's vocational inclinations should not be ignored but solved by making it a source of progressive development. This demands that both economic planning bodies and the school system pay constant attention to the whole complex of objective and subjective factors which have an impact on the integration of youth into the work force.

Sometimes it is said that socialism has no employment problem. This is not the case: all socialist countries face this problem; the socialisation of the means of production just created the possibility to solve the problem in a planned order. In analysing employment problems it is therefore necessary to take other factors into account. Among these, the developments in science and technology as well as in the demographic structure of society are of special relevance.

The development of science and technology follows its own rules, oblivious to humanistic goals and concepts of good or justice. However, new generations entering the work force set new, and higher, demands on the conditions and content of work. They want these conditions to be constantly improved upon, so that work will give them possibilities for creativity, self-realisation and professional growth.

Scientific-technical progress changes the structure of the social division of labour, but, at the same time, it is sometimes quicker at changing the attitude towards professions of physical work. The vocational aspirations of youth show that young people tend to strive for professions of prestigious intellectual work. Because of this, a whole group of professions which are necessary for the economy as a whole are not popular with the young. As a result, developments in science and technology are used to reduce the demand for the manual professions which lack prestige. This occurs with such developments as robot-operated assembly lines.

Demographic developments create a special situation for a person's choice of employment or profession. They influence the opportunities offered to different groups of young people receiving this or that kind of education, the possibility to occupy this or that job, and even the degree of optimism among the different generations of young men and women. The demographic situation, in turn, depends upon the events of the distant past. The consequences of the World War II continue to affect the generations and aggravate the problem of employment resources, especially in the second half of the 1980s. The post-war period shows three phases of population growth. During the first fifteen years, there was an absolute increase of 14.8 million people; during the second fifteen-year-period, the growth constituted 30 million; and during the last fifteen years, it was 5 million.

These sharp fluctuations in population growth are not only connected with changes in the number of those who enter employment (that is, those who reach age twenty), but also with changes in the number of those who leave employment (reaching retirement age). The biggest increase, which took place in the second half of the 1970s, was caused by the coincidence of two events in time: the most populous Soviet generation born at the end of the 1950s entered the work force, at the time when the comparatively less populous generation born in the years of the First World War and the subsequent Soviet Civil War (1916-1920) left the ranks of the employed.

In the second half of the 1980s, the age of twenty will be reached by a relatively small generation, the children of the generation born during the World War II; while the generation born in the second half of the 1920s, which was more populous from the start and which suffered less during the World War II, will be leaving the sector of the gainfully employed.

The diminishing employed population will influence the supply of manpower much sharper (especially now in the twelfth five-year-period) than was the case in the first half of the 1960s. The problem is that the source of worker supply has changed drastically. The young generation has become the major source of supply, while just twenty years ago the manpower requirements of the economy could still be satisfied by bringing in the rural population.

The present decline of the demographic wave in the Soviet Union is taking place against the background of a general decline in birth rates in such areas as the Russian Federation, the Ukraine, the Baltic republics and Byelorussia. This inevitably leads to a drastic reduction in the quantity of young people entering the workforce. And, since all sources are used, the coming years will entail an acute shortage of manpower in the Soviet Union. In some areas, in fact, in order to provide the necessary level of agricultural production, the transition from the city to the countryside is needed.

What this all means is that the new generation of youth should take on an additional work burden in comparison with the previous generation. If a great inertia of economic planning is taken into account - and this is expressed in preserving given volumes, rates and proportions of development - this will inevitably increase competition among industrial branches and regions for manpower, thus putting the young in a position of having to make complicated decisions. Even if the numbers of those who want to enter colleges, technical and vocational schools remain the same, their opportunities to enroll in educational establishments will be increased and probably a greater share of the young will also be able to prolong their studies. On the other hand, the question of how to provide for an uninterrupted functioning of the economy and to attract a greater number of young people for work in industry, agriculture, construction, and transport will be acute. These two directions will certainly compete with each other.

After graduating from school, a new period of life begins when the young men and women come into contact with real social institutions, among them, industrial organisation. This is a period of intensive social maturement and a time when the young review their stereotypes. A comparison of the views of the same young adults at the ages of seventeen and twenty-five shows considerable differences in their estimates of the prestige accorded to professions. When we list the scores given professions by seventeen year-olds of those allotted the highest prestige to those with the lowest prestige, then the curve shows a sharp angle. Eight years later this curve tends to be less angular, as if avoiding extremes. The professions associated primarily with scholarships (in such fields as mathematics, physics, chemistry) and given the highest scores for prestige fell on the scale, while those professions with the lowest scores for prestige (waiter, cook, sales clerk) went up. Surely, the gap between the polar groups of professions is still large, but it is substantially reduced.

Contradictions between aspirations and society's requirements when supply is higher than demand

The situation in many western countries is characterised by a conflict between the qualitative manpower requirements of society and the professional aspirations of youth: an excess of supply over demand, leading to high levels of unemployment, especially among the youth.

Consequently, the problem of a lack of coincidence between the professional aspirations of the young and the needs of society is not only shared with socialist countries, but in many respects, it seems to be conditioned by the specific features of age and by the peculiarities of modern development.[5] The conclusion is the same when the materials prepared by West European sociologists for the present study are analysed. The West European reports clearly indicate that the work expectations of youth have changed, and that in many cases they pose higher demands concerning their work.

The conclusions reached about the lack of correspondence between aspirations of the young and the demands of society for manpower show that this lack of correspondence is caused by the conflict between changed value orientations (in comparison with the older generation) and the conditions of work. This research indicates that the modern organisation of work has been practically unchanged within the last decades, a result of which is that work does not correspond to the expectations and aspirations of the young workforce. Also, although the organisation of work today differs from the methods of classical Taylorism, various studies demonstrate that work has become aimless, fragmentated and stupefying for many workers.

It would, however, be an oversimplification to assume that the young do not accept just such conditions of work which the older generations became 'accustomed' to. There are grounds to presume that the application of modern, scientific-technical achievements to work organisation has made the conflict between youth's expectations and work conditions more pronounced. Rapid technological change has aggravated this situation and the rigidities and greater control of workers imposed by technology has evoked an adverse reaction among young people.[6]

In many countries of Western Europe, the gap between the expectations of the young and the reality of society is compensated for by filling the vacancies in professions of low prestige with migrants from other countries of the world. As a result, the upper part of the pyramid is occupied by native workers, while the base is occupied by immigrant workers. This has serious socio-psychological consequences. The young people of the home country strengthen their alien attitude towards professions of low prestige as they look down at them as not fitting 'their' national origin. At the same time, the attitude that some professions are 'inferior' spreads to the immigrant workers who perform these jobs and they are treated as being 'inferior'. At the same time, social barriers which limit the vertical mobility of young migrants along the pyramid of the professions are solidified by national discrimination. This increases the feeling of alienation generally experienced by migrants and provides the ground for national, racial and ethnic conflicts.

Moreover, the filling of vacancies in professions of low prestige by migrant workers is now taking place under conditions of limited demand on the labour market.

The problem of unemployment has become one of the most acute problems of modern youth in the capitalist countries. Returning to our model of two pyramids, we have a situation in which the size of the pyramid which symbolises society's manpower requirements is considerably more narrow when compared to the size of the 'dotted' pyramid, which symbolises the professions the young want to follow. This means that society can not only satisfy manpower requirements with quality, but also with quantity.

A considerable number of unemployed youth energetically seek jobs, but the lengthy periods this job search involves makes many of them apathetic, and can make them eventually cease looking for work. The situation of chronic unemployment not only changes the professional aspirations of youth - their demands regarding the conditions of work - but also changes their attitude towards work as a way of life in general.

The adverse situation in the sphere of work makes young people who have high demands on the content of work lower those demands to fulfil the simplest requirement: work as a source of subsistence. Here we have a paradoxical situation: along with the tendency to downgrade the importance of income as a motive for work, which is a result of equating work importance with professions of high prestige, there is a trend to upgrade the material factor since, under conditions of unemployment, any work as a source of subsistence is preferable to no work.

While changing value assessments, unemployment considerably changes the professional aspirations of young people as well. On the one hand, as was shown by M.-V. Louis in her study 'Attitudes of Young French Unemployed Youth towards Work' (1984), those young unemployed who have once worked and then lost their job take this change in their status close to heart. These unemployed are 'ashamed of their jobless situations'; it is the reason why many then lose habitual connections with society and the world at large.[7]

On the other hand, the youth who have not had work experience and those who either view themselves as being unable to get a job or who do not want to accept 'any' job (which is usually a job performed by migrant workers) acquire active 'anti-work' psychologies. The criticism of some obsolete forms of work organisation develops into active aversion to any kind of work. Some of the young French unemployed questioned by Louis stated: 'Work is boring. Work is not adapted to life - to the possibility of living. Work is a burden.'[8]

According to Ludevid, increase of unemployment among young Spaniards, has resulted in different attitudes towards unemployment than have been observed among young people twenty years ago. 'Unemployment is no longer considered to be an isolated happenstance of short duration: it is viewed as something inevitable which must be taken into account when planning the future. This change in attitude has influenced the attitude towards work in general, and young people now tend to adapt to chronic unemployment and even to the question whether it is in itself, a negative phenomenon and whether work really deserves to be enshrined as an ideal the way it was in the past'.[9]

It is largely because of unemployment that work has lost its role as a socialising agent of the young. Many young people cease to treat work as a fundamental value and the principle means to happiness and self-realisation.

High unemployment, along with a growing division between youth's expectations and the reality of many jobs, has led to profound changes in values. The age-old work ethic of society is giving way to a leisure ethic. Working youth today divides its life into two entirely separated parts: work (an activity which is often more looked down upon) and 'real' life (which they feel is the only life even worth living).[10]

All this demonstrates that the reduction in demand over supply aggravates even more the growing contradictions between the aspirations of the young and the needs of society.

Conclusions

After this analysis of contradictions in the period of transition from school to work, there are grounds to return to the question which was posed at the beginning of the chapter: how is it possible to achieve an optimal correspondence between the dotted-line and dense-line pyramids - between the manpower needs of society and the professional aspirations of youth?

The first idea that comes to mind is to change the dotted-line pyramid. Here, it is necessary to take the cardinal differences between these processes as they develop in different countries into account. Often sociologists and politicians hope to solve this problem by manipulating the dotted-line pyramid - that is, by using television, the press and the educational system in their interests. But as powerful as the mass media are, they are not almighty. Ultimately, subtle propaganda tries in vain to make people think differently when the matters in question are such urgent problems as the lack of guarantees for employment and the situation of continuing education.

The logic of this analysis demands the return to the first pyramid, which reflects the structure of vacancies. Indeed, is it possible to influence this structure, and, if so, then how? The transformation of the similar structure may involve its reconstruction either vertically or horizontally. The prestige accorded to professions belongs to the sphere of social consciousness, it is very strongly connected with economic life and reflects the character of the existing system of social relations.

That is why the liquidation of such a hierarchy of occupations, the radical transformation of scales of prestige, turns out to be a very complicated task.

The socialisation of basic means of production is an important prerequisite for a change in the prestige scale. The hierarchy of occupations does not automatically change with this, but, as a result of radical transformations in a society, possibilities for a conscious and planned change in the needs for manpower in different professions appear. In other words, the prerequisites for fruitful influence on the system of the social division of labour are created. This makes it possible to reduce, and in some cases to eliminate, the least prestigious professions completely, thus subordinating material conditions to the radical needs, interests and striving of the employed.

This does not mean, however, that society may change the dense-line pyramid at will; it will be a process of gradual adaptation of the structure of social division of labour to the structure of needs and striving of the population.

The setting up of such tasks puts serious demands on those social institutions which take upon themselves the complicated mission to consciously regulate social processes which had before developed on the basis of spontaneous regulators. The necessary condition for such a regulation is a broad development of the natural, technical and social sciences.

This is, however, only the first necessary step. In order to provide for a correspondence between the needs of society and young people's inclinations, it is also necessary to create an effective system of social and professional guidance. Without this, society would not be able to render the needed assistance to young adults at the beginning of their working life. This is exactly one of the goals of the present reform of the secondary and vocational school systems which is taking place in the Soviet Union. It aims to provide the level of knowledge which is necessary to continue studies at school and, at the same time, to guide young people in the direction of socially useful labour in the economy as well as to prepare them for this.

Notes

1. The problem of the vocational aspirations of youth has been the focal point of the 'Project 17-17' study - devoted to the problems of education, vocational choice and youth employment - conducted in the

province of Novosibirsk and some other areas of the Soviet Union in 1963. The same problem was dealt with in 1983 in the 'Twenty Years Later' project (which used the same methods as the 1963 project) when the graduates of Novosibirsk were the subject of a survey. This survey made it possible to investigate the dynamics of the employment problems and the vocational choice of youth over a long period of time (twenty years) and to make a comparative analysis of the change of two generations. See, V. Shubkin, *Soziologicheskie opyty*, (Moscow, 1970); V. Shubkin, *Nachalo pouty: Problemy molodezhi v zerkale soziologii y literatury* (Beginning of the path: the problems of youth in the mirror of sociology and works of fiction), (Moscow, 1979); F. Gazsó and V. Shubkin (eds), *Trudyashayasya molodezh: orientazii y zhiznenie pouty. Opyt sravnitelnogo sociologicheskogo issledovania* (Working youth: orientation and life path. Experiment of comparative sociological study), (Budapest, 1980); G. Cherednichenko and V. Shubkin, *Molodezh vstupaet v zhizn Molodzh vstupaet v zhizn* (Youth enter life), (Moscow, 1985).

2. W. Adamski, *Education and Careers in Today's Poland*, (European Institute of Educational and Social Policy, Amsterdam, 1983).

3. P.E. Mitev *et al., Youth and Labour*, (Sofia, 1983a).

4. G. Cherednichenko and V. Shubkin, *Molodezh vstupaet v zhizn*, (Moscow, 1985), pp. 62-3.

5. Y.V. Emeljanov, *Obostrenie sozialno-politicheskih protivorechii v SShA y molodezh*, (Moscow, 1986), pp. 54-5.

6. H. Stegmann, 'Analysis of changes and differences in the attitudes and behaviour of young people towards work', in: P. Grootings (ed.), *Youth and Work in Europe* (Vienna Centre-Moscow, Moscow, 1984), vol. II, p. 90.

7. M.-V. Louis, 'Attitudes of young French unemployed towards work', in: P.Grootings (ed), *Youth and Work in Europe* (Vienna Centre-Moscow, Moscow, 1984), vol. I, p. 151.

8. M.-V. Louis, ibid., p. 153.

9. M. Ludevid, 'Young People and Work in Spain', in: P. Grootings (ed.), *Youth and Work in Europe* (Vienna Centre-Moscow, Moscow, 1984), vol. II, pp. 88-101.

10. P. Grootings (ed.), *Youth and Work in Europe* (Vienna Centre-Moscow, Moscow, 1984), vol. 1, p. 96.

4

Changing Values and the Transition from School to Work

Rose-Marie Greve, Ilan Knapp, Fred Mahler,
Gustavo de Santis and Anna-Maria Ventrella

Introduction

As a decisive step towards adulthood, the transition from school to work is one of the more crucial phases in the psycho-social development of young people. Characterised by the massive confrontation of the expectations, needs, wishes and value orientations (engendered by the family, school and the peer group) with the realities of the world of work, the period of transition sometimes affords opportunities for internal and external conflict, thus making entry into working life a key event in the development of the personality during which values (both general and work specific) undergo considerable change. Explicitly or implicitly, values are an essential feature of the process of transition and of each of its individual sequences. They are thus a basic component of the transition of young people from school to work and their analysis is a *sine qua non* of the present study.

On the basis of Merton's theory of anticipatory socialisation, one might suggest that the transformation of 'learning' into 'working' values through an appropriate process of value change is a prerequisite for the transformation of young people from educational social actors to productive social actors. Both as individuals and as groups, young people have particular value orientations concerning school and society which influence their vocational aspirations and value choices. These, in turn, influence their paths in life. In addition, their behaviour upon entering the work process is a reflection of ingrained value orientations *vis-à-vis* professions and productive setting.

However, it must be noted that, as a concept, 'values' is vague, ambiguous and difficult to define in a scientifically accurate and unequivocal manner. Kluckhohn, for example, provides a definition which captures 'the fluid state of value studies ... and the ambiguity of the term value' when he contends that 'a value is a conception, explicit or implicit, distinctive of an individual or characteristic of a group, of the desirable which influences the selection from the available modes, means and ends of action'. In fact, values express the relationship between environmental pressures and human desires and since they 'represent a meeting point between the individual and society, value research is potentially well suited to explore cross-cultural variations within an interdisciplinary framework by articulating the goals of cultural anthropology, sociology and psychology' (Kluckhohn, 1951). Thus the concept offers the present project a useful opportunity to grasp the 'unity in diversity' which characterises the complex, multiform and often contradictory process that comprises the transition of young people from school to work within the context of an interdisciplinary, holistic, dynamic and critical international perspective.

On a theoretical level and on the basis of empirical research, this chapter addresses the question of whether young people have, in fact, changed or are changing their attitudes and behaviour towards work; and, if this is the case, what are or may be the consequences of these changes on the period of transition from school to work as well as on the resulting 'mismatch'. The second section focuses on the theoretical dimension. The socio-psychological approach adopted as a means to answer these questions gives both the general framework and the different levels necessary to refer to in order to understand the work value orientations of young people in the 1980s.

The third section is to summarise those ideas which emerged at the international workshops (Moscow, Sofia, Castelgandolfo, Barcelona, Lauf and Vienna) regarding the empirical evidence which may support or reject the hypothesis that there is a radical shift in work values among youth.

The final section offers some alternative answers to the following questions: What are the present work values of the employed population as a whole? Which of these are work values accepted by the young? What are the consequences of youth's work-value orientations for the transition from school to work? The congruency (or lack of it) between the theoretical model and the empirical findings offers some insights for a better scientific approach of this topic altogether and some suggestions for practical improvement of youth transition from school to work.

The Theoretical Dimension: A Socio-Psychological Approach to the Change in Young People's Work-Value Orientations

As was noted earlier, the change in values and attitudes is a highly complex process in which a number of cultural, political, social and personal factors interact. Our analysis covers both the *exogenous* and *endogenous* dimensions of this interrelationship. the exogenous dimension refers to all structures, including their value orientations, which are 'exterior' to youth and which shape young people's value orientations and behaviour, both in general and towards work, through socialisation, education and integration processes. The endogenous dimension refers to the needs, aspirations, value orientations and behaviour of youth - to the specific structural peculiarities of youth, such as age and gender. Clearly, any exact separation between the 'external' and the 'internal' dimensions of youth versus the general value orientations and behaviour of society is only analytic and can only be considered to be a methodological tool with limited explanatory power.

The following presentation has two theoretical parts, the analysis of which is then applied to the empirical research and its conclusions. When the exogenous dimension requires a more *sociologically* oriented approach and the endogenous dimension a more *psychological* one - both approaches will be used almost concomitantly. Emphasis is, however, on the endogenous dimension for two reasons: first, because exogenous factors determine the genesis, structure, content and evolution of the endogenous factors and an understanding of the former is crucial to an understanding of the latter; and second, because social phenomena are 'context-bound' or 'systemic' deriving their meaning from the contexts in which they occur.

The Exogenous Dimension

The focus of this section is on social systems and their subsystems (e.g. education, employment, labour market, culture, socialisation agencies, normative and axiological social factors and processes, demographic trends, etc.) and will include an analysis of their interrelationships and of macro-, meso- and micro-level peculiarities.

It is obvious that the individual value orientations of young people are not the result of solipsistic or aleatoric products but are rather the result of a complex process of value transmission and change. This process takes place at various levels: the *macro* level (nation, state, political and economic systems, social classes, internal and international division of labour, culture and society as a whole), the *meso* level (social groups, institutionalised socialising agencies such as school, productive units, and the formal and informal labour force) and the *micro* level (family, peer groups and informal interpersonal relations). While, in one sense, the interrelationship between these three levels of factors makes their isolation somewhat artificial, it is, nevertheless, a useful distinction, in that it permits the analysis of the different value orientations within and between these different factors, and it highlights the fact that their influence on the individual is not necessarily congruent. It also permits the examination of the wide range of contradictions which arise when the value orientations engendered by different factors, at the different levels, influence young people's values and behaviour, and when this exogenous pressure meets endogenous factors. In this context, it should also be noted that individuals, as social groups with their own values, beliefs and behaviours, themselves play an active role in the process of value change.

The Macro Level

The analysis of value change at the macro level often comes up against a very basic contradiction, namely, that the necessity for a generalised model as a research tool is in direct contradiction to the real situation which is far too complex, variable and dynamic - a single abstraction is not sufficiently sensitive to the diversity of scientific and axiological approaches, or to the fundamental differences which exist between and within countries.

An axiom of the approach used in this study has been a recognition of the fact that while the countries concerned share many common features, the many, and sometimes fundamental, differences which exist within and among them must not be lost sight of. On an intercountry level, the various stages of economic development and the form and content they take in different social and political systems is an important issue; dominant value orientations, including the work ethic as reflected in social norms and day-to-day behaviour, is another. Within countries one can point out, for example, that modern societies are highly differentiated, comprising a number of social strata each subject to different opportunities and conditions of life and each, therefore, with different needs, interests, values and attitudes. The considerable mobility between the strata may be both the reason for, and the object of, the various value orientations. There is also a high degree of differentiation within the subsystems of social life (e.g. the political, economic and cultural systems; the educational system; leisure; consumption patterns; etc.). Although these subsystems are in close interaction, their specific circumstances and structures result in different value conceptions, giving rise to a number of areas of conflict which, in turn, contribute to the dynamism of value systems as a whole.

Nevertheless, on a global level, it can be argued, and has been argued, that in Europe as a whole, the macro-social background of the transition from school to work and the value change it implies should be viewed within the context of a shift from an industrial to a post-industrial society. The concomitant macro-value system is that of a new post-materialistic work ethic, which, it is suggested, has superseded the traditional materialistic value system of the classical industrial society. Basically, this theory contends that the unprecedented economic growth and its positive social repercussions (epitomised in the concept of full employment and in the creation of the welfare state) has permitted societies to look beyond the basic needs of life to other human needs and aspirations (such as leisure, self-realisation, creativity and human relations), and that youth has been the main agent of change in the process.

While it has much to recommend it, this theory must nonetheless be viewed with caution given the diversity and complexity of existing socio-economic situations and trends within and among European countries. Certainly not all European countries have entered the post-industrial era; and many are characterised by the co-existence of pre-industrial, industrial and post-industrial characteristics, all of which impact differentially on the process of transition from school to work. In addition, one must take account of the different shape development takes on in socialist or capitalist countries, in centrally planned or market economies, and at national and local levels.

Even more controversial than the influence of the present stage of development on the macro determinants of the process of value changes is the issue of future trends towards the 'post-industrial' (or 'affluent', 'welfare', 'active', 'achieving', 'technotonic', 'self-service', 'caring', 'mass-consumption', 'third wave', etc.) society. Not only are there terminological differences but also basic, axiological and socio-politically opposed views.

Thus, while the post-industrial theory with its related post-material value system could, and does, apply to some countries, it cannot be considered to be a unique explanation of value change in contemporary society. Baethge suggests that the 'claim that materialistic value orientations are being supplanted by post-materialist ones is ... based on an inadequate methodological approach' and that, in any event 'one finds that the so-called "materialist" values-orientation was clearly dominant in all West European countries (included in the study) during the period in question, the 1970s' (Baethge, 1984).

Other research models of value change have also been developed and tested in Europe. For example, surveys focusing on work motivation and the system of 'exogenous' and 'endogenous' influences on it have been carried out in Italy and constitute a good example of efforts to study the macro value determinants of the transition process using such indicators as the quality of life, job quality and the instrumentality of work. While these and other empirical studies in Eastern and Western Europe demonstrate the differences in theoretical and methodological approaches, they all underline the importance of the macro level in shaping the value orientations of youth in the transition process, youth's eventual work motivations, youth's educational and vocational aspirations and the choices and alternatives effected during the process of integration.

Thus, research in market economy countries suggests that class values are one of the main factors which mediate between the status young people ascribe to and the status which they achieve. For example, Bourdieu suggests that class bias affects the development of vocational values and aspirations through the mechanism of the self-limitation of career possibilities in the light of perceptions of a 'probable future' defined along class lines and common to all members of the same class status. Similarly, Bernstein underlines the values built into the 'invisible' school curricula and the class differences between educational codes and their consequences for professional and social mobility.

In centrally planned economies, empirical evidence demonstrates that while class membership is no longer the main differentiating factor in the value orientations, aspirations and vocational careers of young people, it still has some consequences in that residence (with a very real gap between urban and rural areas), the educational background of families and other cultural factors are more decisive than nominal class membership.

The Meso and Micro Levels

Studies of value changes during the transition from school to work underline the convergence of contradictions between individual value orientations and the dominant value orientation, i.e. the work ethic of a given society, at a particular stage of its development. Individual value orientations are shaped in their specific macro context by the influence of meso factors such as social classes and social groups as well as the institutionalised socialising agencies (e.g. schools, production systems, etc.) and micro factors such as the family and peer groups.

In all countries, the school system plays an important role in the development of values and attitudes and in the resulting behavioural consequences. In market economies, the complex relationship between the macro and meso factors influencing the values of young people in the transition process are reflected in the part played by the structure of the school system which separates post primary students into two streams - vocational and academic - with two sets of work ethics, two kinds of vocational aspirations and two different patterns of integration and mobility. In fact, aside from the family at the micro level, the school system has become one of the most important avenues of socialisation and for shaping youth's value orientations. Its importance has also grown considerably given that increasing numbers of young people tend to stay in school longer, a sort of 'prolonged adolescence' which could constitute the basis of a more differentiated and independent personality development, especially in view of the recent changes in teaching methods which stress creativity, self-determination and participation.

At the same time, with reference to the market economy countries, the family (and its social background) constitutes the primary influence on young people's initial value orientations towards school and work although other factors (such as the social environment, peer subculture and the mass media message) also have an impact on the process. Once in a given stream at school, the previous value set - possibly engendered by micro factors - interacts with a specific school value system which, while it is either convergent or divergent, together creates a new set of value orientations. A new stage begins when this sequence of value change ends with graduation, and when integration into the employment system requires new value changes. As a third step in the process (the family and the school system influencing the first two), the employment system assumes a primary influence over young people's value orientations which may well be subjected to change in order to adapt to the demands of the new setting. In this context, it needs to be noted that the changes in job profiles and skill demands engendered by technological and organisational change, and the consequent emphasis on polyvalence, has given rise to a need for life-long education, thus blurring the traditional borders between school/education on the one hand and work/occupation on the other. In addition, traditional authority and decision-making structures in enterprises are being called increasingly into question by the growing technical and social competence of employees and may have to change in response to this development, thus bringing the organisation of the work place and its value system closer to that of the 'ideal' educational system.

Scholars in the educational field in the socialist countries also suggest that meso and micro 'exogenous' values influence the individual value orientations of young people in specific ways. Despite new characteristics which compare with experiences in other countries, this process continues to be a contradictory one because the expected convergence between socialisation factors at the micro and meso levels has yet to be achieved fully and automatically; there is a distance, if not a gap, between postulated and real value orientations as the latter are manifested in behaviour in specific educational and work settings; and when set against the work ethics and the normative axiological system as a whole, individual value orientations and even the school- and work-related values of families, peer groups and other informal communities are often different. As Shubkin points out, a 'real contradiction in the process of choosing a profession is arising between society's requirements in trained personnel and young people's vocational preferences for particular careers' (Shubkin, 1984).

In general terms, and from a sociological point of view, the exogenous aspect of the value orientations of young people in the context of their transition from school to work necessitates an analysis of the relationship between the individual's value orientations and those of the different factors at micro, meso and macro levels as well as the study of their own isomorphisms or differences in specific social settings and in a diachronic way.

The Endogenous Dimension

The value orientation of young people towards work has its own, endogenous dimension, which is influenced, to an important degree, by exogenous factors. First, this value orientation is an expression of those patterns of value orientations, and of the resulting behaviour patterns associated with a given age, i.e. with the stages of an individual's psychosomatic, intellectual, and moral development. A second trait is gender, which is the basis for specific ways young individuals commit to values in general and to work in particular.

Apart from the constantly changing societal, social and cultural conditions, a further important factor in the dynamics of changing values can be found in the process of growing up, i.e. the transition from childhood to adulthood. Each society is constantly faced with the problem of educating and integrating succeeding generations in an adequate manner which corresponds to the specific conditions of the society concerned and needs to convey norms and values which secure the continued existence and functioning of society while making life within the community possible for each individual member of society. Within this process, the norms and values are subject to re-interpretation and a certain pressure of legitimation on the part of young. In this way the norms and values are constantly actualising the relativity and contradictory nature of such systems and accordingly causing changes in the value system. These changes may mean an adaptation to new societal, social and cultural conditions, but they may also contradict prevailing values and aim at changing existing conditions.

The endogenous values most frequently associated with the present changes in youth's value orientations are generally (and perhaps erroneously) subsumed under the title of 'post materialist' values and associated with the 'post industrial' society referred to earlier. While acknowledging the shortcomings of this theoretical construct, it is worth noting that many of the values attributed to it are indeed surfacing in many European countries.

As was noted earlier, the satisfaction of the basic (physical) needs of working populations has permitted them to pay greater attention to their psychological needs and to look to the satisfaction of these needs within the various social and economic systems and sub-systems. Thus, leisure, self-realisation, creativity, interpersonal relations and cultural and aesthetic needs appear to assume greater importance among young people and are expressed in their attitudes and behaviour in various macro, meso and micro settings (e.g. society, the school and work). In the societal setting, these preoccupations manifest themselves, for example, in concern for the environment and for macro level problems such as poverty, peace and democracy. Educational systems are frequently criticised for their emphasis on competition rather than cooperation and for their authoritarian instrumental student-teacher relationships and the consequent lack of opportunities for personality development. In this context, it is noteworthy that, in some countries, these criticisms have constituted one catalyst in the revision of educational systems to allow for greater attention to the ideas, expectations and interests of students.

In view of the importance of work to the study of value change in the context of the transition process, protagonists of the 'new work ethic' argue that work has changed its meaning and that young people bring a different set of needs, expectations and values to their jobs than those of previous generations. While this contention is based largely on survey data, which has its limitations, it is nevertheless worth noting that, in general terms, it is claimed that work is no longer regarded merely as a means of earning money for life outside working hours but becomes an integral part of life and personality. Professional aspirations expand to encompass values such as creativity, self-realisation, interpersonal relations, responsibility and participation; in so doing, they are often in direct conflict with the existing work situation which is largely characterised by hierarchical relations, authoritarian decision-making and technological determinism.

As the earlier discussion has emphasised, it cannot be claimed that such values are shared by all young people, and it is evident that exogenous factors and life experience play an important role in shaping both values and their behavioural manifestations. Youth is not a homogeneous group and its subgroups may well have different value orientations and behaviours. For example, as was noted in the discussion of exogenous meso factors, the dual system in the school system existing in market economies results in the creation of different value orientations, aspirations and behaviours. To these two groups of youth, one can add two other groups whose educational and work experience differ considerably from that of students in the formal system already mentioned, with inevitable consequences for their aspirations and value orientations. The first group comprise apprentices, characterised by an early adoption of work-related patterns of behaviour and by a disciplined integration into a complex work process. The second is that of drop-outs with no post primary education of either a vocational or an academic nature. With the decrease in demand for unskilled or semi-skilled workers brought about by technological and organisational change, these young people are most likely to be found among the unemployed or marginal groups in the labour market and to have their own sub-culture based on a set of values that differ from those of both post primary school students and apprentices. Differentiation can also have an intergenerational dimension and values can differ from one age group or cohort to another. Altogether, it is probable that empirical research would uncover a mix - or rather mixes - of material and post material values among different groups of young people. In sum, perhaps the most striking fact which emerges from this discussion of endogenous factors is their close interrelationships with exogenous factors by which they are shaped and which they, in turn, reshape.

Empirical Research: Methods and Problems

It is a general belief that a comparative analysis on this theme is very difficult, and that, as a consequence, there are serious limits to the results attained. In addition to obstacles and difficulties of a general nature, there are also those related to the specific question under consideration. The theme of the meaning of work and, more generally, the work ethic (regarded as a bundle of values, beliefs, intentions and objectives that people bring to their work and the conditions in which they do it) are difficult to define. Clarke tackling this question in an international overview, rightly observed that 'the great difference between countries, social systems, tradition and degree of industrial development compound the difficulties'. He added that 'there is no agreed form of measurement reflecting the work ethic itself or even its major components. There is a lack of comparability among most of those indicators which might be thought to yield at least secondary evidence. And the work ethic itself forms only a part of the wide-ranging systems of values which people hold individually and demonstrate in their wider societal relationship' (Clarke, 1985).

The crucial points identified (especially by Baethge, 1984 and Wilpert, 1984) concern:

- the definition of 'youth' - since this is not a homogeneous

social group but rather a reality with sex, age, scholastic education and vocational or professional training, labour market conditions, family origin, and other specific traits;
- the heterogeneous nature of the methodological approaches followed;
- the unsatisfactory quality of the investigations owing to the level of abstraction of some items, the small number thereof in relation - for example - to attitudes, the subjective interpretation and evaluation of the data, the diversity in the formulation of the items in subsequent studies, etc.;
- more generally, the inadequacy and lack of comparability of official statistical sources.

Apart from these specific critical points, there are others whose significance is such as to throw serious doubts on any evaluation or judgment made on the basis of these investigations. But as these are connected to the same theoretical approach followed in the observation of young people's value change, it is more useful to come back to them in the final paragraph.

Youth's Work Values: the Empirical Evidence

The aim of this paragraph is to summarise, against the background of the theoretical model sketched before, empirical evidence that may help answer the basic question: has there been a change in the work values of young people?

It will become apparent that it is precisely empirical evidence and theoretical-methodological reflections on the investigations made in various countries which raise legitimate doubts as to whether a question posed in these terms can be answered today in a completely unequivocal manner. There are certainly many signals that can be used for the purpose, but these are often ambiguous, or even contradictory. Yet everyone is certain about one point, namely, that something is changing or has already changed, both in the East and the West, with effects appearing in the relationship between the individual and work. It is not clear, however, whether the changes have occurred mainly (or perhaps exclusively) among the youth, nor is it clear whether they mark a complete break with the past. But what does seem to be the case from the empirical encounters is the existence of differences in attitudes and behaviour of individuals *vis-à-vis* work and on the labour market, due to endogenous and exogenous factors that result in variations in the population as a whole and in specific age subgroups.

The points made are of an extremely synthetic nature, being the result of careful analysis of the various contributions available and the additional investigations and reflections concerning each individual national situation. They do, however, lead to the idea of organizing the investigatory work indicated at the beginning so as to cover three crucial aspects: the explanatory capacity of empirical research on the topic 'values and attitudes regarding work', the work values of youth and the differences among the various subgroups (among these are: the young and not-so-young, the young belonging to various age groups, those belonging to different socio-economic and political systems and those with different educational and vocational backgrounds.

Indicators of Change in Work Values

There is a general consensus that 'young people's attitudes and behaviour patterns associated with work are somehow changing' (Baethge, 1985). This and similar statements are prompted by a multitude of signals, not all of which are homogeneous, emerging from investigations on the values and behaviour of the population as a whole, as well as of particular subgroups, including youth.

A first check - albeit indirect - on change in the work relationship is provided for by observing the growing dissatisfaction with work over the last ten or fifteen years. This concerns both the population in general (as exemplified by the West German data) and the subgroups (as indicated, for instance, in the Italian case by reference to the employees, with a breakdown between young and old).

Assuming that work satisfaction can be seen as an indirect indicator of work orientation, this trend would appear to be explained by the change in aspirations regarding work conditions and in the new concept of work in which work is seen more as a chance than an obligation (Wilpert, 1984). Furthermore, the fact that older people see work more as an obligation than an opportunity, and that this trend does not vary linearly with age, would tend to indicate that changes in work values are occurring in the population as a whole - although with differences among the various age groups. Clear confirmation of this is given by the

Italian data which indicate that between 1971 and 1982 there was an increase in those dissatisfied, both among workers as a whole and among young people. And this without having any effect on the relative position of the two groups (De Santis and Ventrella, 1984).

Information on a completely different socio-economic situation such as Finland clearly illustrates trends among the different generations (e.g. between those born at the beginning of the century and those belonging to the post-World War II generations) as regards the meaning of work, the motivations for education, closer human relationships, and so on (Volanen, 1984a).

Coming now more specifically to the present meaning of work, it can be said that there appears to be no decline in significance. Indeed, because of the economic crisis (at least in Western countries), work has become a 'scarce commodity', which may justify, for instance, the situation that a growing number of persons would continue to work even in the presence of a radical positive change in their economic condition (Hövels and Vissers, 1984).

However, while more people opt for work, the conditions in which they would like to work or continue to work differ. For instance, the desire to work shorter hours is expressed by the older section of the population, but without any loss of pay; while youth would prefer shorter hours even with less pay. Then, too, there are differences in attitudes towards work: the traditional one (work as a duty) which is the tenet of the older, skilled, highly paid workers; the concept of work as a right and a source of income, which is held mainly by elderly men with a middling level of education and income; the 'socially oriented' idea, which is less common but more widely held by young people and women; and last, the 'modern' outlook, which is mainly that of youth and of men and women with a high level of education - namely, that while work is seen as a right, it is important not so much from the monetary aspect but because of its instrinsic characteristics and the possibilities it offers for the development of social relationships (Hövels and Vissers, 1984).

Data on the Italian situation confirm the effects of the economic crisis on the value given to work and bear out the change which has taken place in the very concept of work. This change appears widespread throughout the population, in the sense that the trend is towards paying greater attention to the socialising characteristics and interest of work, and this attitude may well be more common among the youth.

Another indirect indicator of change in the attitude towards work - specific to youth in this case - is that the majority believes that education is the best way of attaining a positioi. in society. This indicator, however, has a different value in the various socio-political situations. In Western countries (Spain, for instance, Ludevid, 1984), it would appear as an essential prerequisite to enter into an active life; while in Eastern countries, it would appear to be the premise for achieving the aspiration of having different jobs and different working conditions from those of one's parents.

Though at first sight, signs of a change in the youth/work relationship in Eastern countries may appear weak and of little significance, they are highly indicative precisely because of the socio-economic context in which they occur. In fact, because of the role of work in the construction of socialist society - the high level of satisfaction in work which appears to emerge from official information and the absence of unemployment - every manifestation of tension revealed by investigations performed in these countries, every change in the attitudes and behaviour of youth, and every preference expressed are elements of proof that there is change: the combined value of these elements is certainly no smaller than the values stemming from those elements observed when considering the situation in the West. Just the fact that studies on young people are being made (on both the national level and on a comparative basis) testifies to the leadership's perception of a change.

One example is provided by the data available on Bulgaria which clearly shows a change in the life principles of the different generations: whereas the life principle of grandparents and parents can still be expressed by the maxim 'Work and save!' irrespective of all the historical modifications of the meaning and content of work and thrift, the life principle of the younger generation can be presented by a new maxim 'Work and enjoy life!' Furthermore, while the moral of life - love of work - comes first in all three generations, in the case of grandparents it has an absolute and general value, while for parents it carries less weight, and for youth this decline is even more marked. In other words, the respect for the principle of the so-called 'abstract love of work' - industriousness irrespective of the proportion of effort put into it and the outcome attained - vanishes in the notions of the new generation. On the rise instead is the importance of the efficiency and quality of work (Mitev, 1983a; 1984). In other Eastern countries, too, there are various signs of growing interest in a different quality of work.

It seems that many of the young - be they Poles, Russians, Rumanians or Czechs - aspire to a creative, interesting job. This aspiration for an 'attractive job' appears to be becoming much more widespread among the youth, though it should be noted that the real data for backing up this idea regarding such a complex, multidimensional concept are still extremely fragmentary. However, research in some countries points out that intellectual work today is perhaps not the most 'attractive'; there could well be other jobs and professions, even though with differences depending on sex and region, as will be seen later (Babushkina, 1985).

There is also, among some youth groups, dissatisfaction with the available work, although this dissatisfaction can be deduced only indirectly. The dissatisfied can be considered to be those who would not opt for their present job if they were free to choose again. This category of person is found in different socialist countries, amounting to around one third in Czechoslovakia, more in Hungary, more again in the Soviet Union and even more in Bulgaria where they represent the majority (Kiuranov, 1985).

Dissatisfaction with the job in question may be bound up with the growing trend towards professional mobility encountered in Czechoslovakia and the Soviet Union in the 1950s (Viteckova and Hudecek, 1984; Babushkina, 1985). Attempts made at the national level (e.g. the Czech plans for the welfare development of labour teams) to curb undesirable fluctuations could be considered to be indicative of contradictions as regards work attitudes. Another sign of this reality may be found in a characteristic situation common to some Eastern countries: the unsatisfactory standards of work performance (Viteckova and Hudecek, 1984).

Work Value and Youth Subgroups

What has been done so far is an attempt to summarise under broad headings the indications of change in work values with reference to youth as a general category. It is necessary to bear in mind, however, the indications which have emerged several times during the course of the work performed by the international group and which are exemplified most specifically and exhaustively in B.

Wilpert's and I. Knapp's contributions. Wilpert (1984) asserts that: 'Before one is able to generalise over a whole generation, it would be necessary to differentiate clearly between various social backgrounds and concrete experience with work life: it appears highly doubtful to lump together such diverse categories as lower-educated youth in prolonged vocational training, university students, skilled unemployed, and members of alternative settings in large cities. Besides, the large majority of 20-30 year-olds are still gainfully employed'.

And then to continue with Knapp (1984a): 'There are great differences not only in the various countries but also between groups within the countries. There are differences in the various school careers open to young people. The problems of young people in the countryside are different from those in the town... there are still great differences between male and female young people. Those between the children from immigrant families and other citizens are increasing'.

Eastern experts are also of this opinion when they say that: 'Youth cannot be considered a homogeneous group. The world of young people is a very composite one and so is the process of their transition from school to work' (Rus and Drobnic, 1985).

Young people with different standards of education and training

One of the first main distinctions is that between the young with specific vocational training and those without: the latter seem to regard work more as an occasional or fortuitous factor; whereas, among the former, choices and rational behaviour would appear to prevail. This would explain the different manner in which the two groups live the work experience and plan their respective careers. But even within the vocational-trainees subgroup there emerge differences connected with possible disillusionment that may have occurred during the training period, especially owing to shortcomings in the training system. In other words, at the end of that period, young people may have acquired different attitudes towards work - disillusionment, resignation or perhaps optimism (Wilpert, 1984).

It has been found everywhere that various attitudes and behaviour *vis-à-vis* work can be tied in with various levels of education. More instrumental attitudes can be tied in with middle-to-low levels of education, while interest for work and the possibility of self-expression comes more frequently with middle-to-high levels of education (Hövels and Vissers, 1984; Hoffman 1985).

Connecting the two aspects of education and vocational training, Knapp reflects on the work attitudes of three different sub-groups of young people (those without vocational training, apprentices and those with secondary education); he also singles out a number of trends.

The first sub-group, whose members once used to opt for immediate entry into the labour market to earn money and become independent, seem to be increasingly oriented towards acquiring a higher standard of education and vocational training, partly because it is difficult to find a job without a higher standard of education. The second, namely the aspiring apprentices - also because of labour market difficulties - are faced not so much with the problem of the type of vocational training to choose but rather of finding a vacancy. A process of adjustment between desired training and possible training would be realised. Moreover, this process would continue even after the individual has entered working life. The third subgroup is distinguished by a high level of education (the number of such people is increasing in the West and - according to Adamski - especially in the East), so they actually start work later in life and hence there is a delay in their acquiring direct work experience. The result is that these young people have to contend for a longer period with personal, social and societal problems at a high level of abstraction. The coexistence of wide margins of freedom from material constraints in this group of young people favours the development of motivations such as: 'self-realisation, initiative, creativity, interesting nature of work, responsibility, participation, etc. ... this means that work and occupation are increasingly considered as an integral component of one's own personality rather than a separate sphere necessary for securing one's material well-being' (Adamski, 1985a).

Education and vocational training also emerge as important factors in Eastern countries. For instance, the development of professional experience, as well as of life experience, reinforces the importance of the social components in the work process. Furthermore, though it is true that during vocational training, or during the initial acquisition of professional experience, the level of aspirations shifts towards socio-professional needs, it is equally true that there are profound differences in the level of congruence between exercised profession and professional aspirations in the various groups of young people. This congruence is less marked among unskilled and semi-skilled manual occupations. That is why there is greater satisfaction over work in what might be defined as areas of intellectual work than in areas of manual work. And it is certainly no coincidence that the least satisfied group of workers includes a large percentage of those workers who have acquired only a basic education (Viteckova and Hudecek, 1984).

In Bulgaria, the data reveal that industriousness is found more widely in the models of personality of the young people with a low standard of education and that 'the lower the educational level, the more frequent is an external attitude to work and an indifference to its content' (Mitev, 1984).

To sum up, in many Eastern countries, it seems true that 'the higher the qualification, the greater the satisfaction with the profession chosen' (Molnar, 1984a).

The jobless youth

Like other classes of workers, jobless youth are apparently motivated more by the desire to have a traditional type of job (namely a stable, secure position) rather than a casual, precarious job (Ludevid, 1984; Louis, 1984). What singles these people out from young workers and young students is the smaller attention paid to the qualitative aspect of the job and a much broader instrumental conception thereof (De Santis and Ventrella, 1984).

Although these are the general lines of the sub-group, they vary depending on education, training and other socio-economic variables. For instance, the well-qualified jobless put forward specific requests, continuing to have a decided preference for a job in keeping with their vocational capabilities.

The less well qualified unemployed, instead, are more disposed to accept - if necessary - a different job from the one they used to have.

The behaviour of these people is thus not determined solely by their state of unemployment but especially by their cultural and vocational background, namely 'the nature of the economic, social and cultural environment' ... as well as 'the effect of the types of social relations'. According to a report on the French situation which is also applicable to various other environments in Western Europe, the jobless can be broken down into three classes. The first can be defined as 'workers deprived of employment'. They form part 'of the class of skilled workers whose culture is strongly marked by work and by the valorisation of professional capacity'. (Louis, 1984)

For this group 'unemployment is experienced as an interruption of the professional and social order which is marked by a working morale'. A second category, defined as 'neither worker nor unemployed', consists of 'jobless people belonging to the middle class or to the deteriorated working class' which, for a variety of reasons, are living in a situation of discrepancy between work and self-fulfilment. A third class groups those who are at the periphery not only of the labour market but more often of the social system, so being jobless is no more than an extension of their exclusion from society and 'the loss of little freedom and of the opening to a world which might have been won by work' (Louis, 1984).

Other sub-groups

So far we have tried to single out major differences in behaviour and attitudes of the young regarding work through two key variables taken by way of example (education and training on the one hand, unemployment on the other). However, although these two variables are certainly highly relevant and can explain much, they are not the only ones that mark distinctions in the world of youth.

Another variable to be considered is the age at which the young people come on the labour market or, to put it another way, to take into account the general widespread delay in the occurrence of entering the labour market which could lead to 'a new phase between adolescence and the status of economically self-sufficient grown-ups' (Wilpert, 1984). This is the phase of post-adolescence, the emergence of which is the result of the theoretical connection between social-structural change and the living conditions of young people. It is clear what the significance may be in terms of the relationship to work - of living through a phase of post-adolescence - when one considers the differences found even now among the young, depending on whether they are students, gainfully employed or jobless (De Santis and Ventrella, 1984).

Another factor influencing a maturation of the ideas of young people regarding work is the process of experimental transition to working life. This process, which certainly includes 'the history of both education and work', can well be considered under one of the four following categories:

- Tubular: quick transition into a job corresponding to education;
- Fan-shaped: work history dispersing, i.e. jobs do not

correspond to education;

- Funnel-shaped: educational history is divided into different fields of education, but work history leads rapidly to a job corresponding to education;
- Comblike: educational history covering several fields and work history dispersing (Volanen, 1984a).

Although this breakdown was made in relation to the specific situation in Finland, it lends itself well to representing what occurs elsewhere.

In other words, the way of transition is the result of a series of variables such as those considered here (education, training, socioeconomic backgrounds - both individual and that of context) and it lies at the origin of attitudes and behaviour and of the way these change.

Gender is also an explanatory variable because, even with the reduction in differences between males and females, there still exist peculiarities in the relationship of young men and women to work. In brief, women continue to follow certain educational channels and lines of training (Knapp, 1984a; Molnar, 1984a); they still have a more difficult transition than men; and they still enter the labour market at a lower level. Combined with the persisting family role of the woman, this leads to a specific culture of work as regards the way of entering it, the vocational preferences, jobs, etc. All this leads to women paying more attention than men to characteristics referable to the quality of life; they are less interested in job quality, but, and it is not only a coincidence, they find themselves in line with men when they manifest instrumental orientations (De Santis and Ventrella, 1984). This typical nature of the female component of the young labour force is also found in the Eastern countries, for instance, as regards vocational preferences, insertion on the labour market and interaction between the social role and the family role (Babushkina, 1985; Molnar, 1984a; Dinkova, 1984).

The factors considered so far, together with others which we have not dwelt on for reasons of brevity, contribute, altogether, to creating the differences found in young people's relationship to work and which can be referred to as the 'local situation' to which young people belong.

In fact, on passing from the supernational level to that of the nation and region, differences are observed, for instance, between young people from the East and those from the West, between

those from countries with different levels of industrialisation and
of development in general, and so on.

There is no lack of empirical examples for this state of affairs,
even though profound differences emerge between the East and
the West in regard to the level of knowledge. The most
enlightening example is provided by the international study on six
countries of Eastern Europe (Mitev, 1983b). The adopted
comparative approach permits many theoretical and
methodological reflections whose value goes far beyond that
socio-political system (Adamski, 1985a; Shubkin, 1984). For the
Western countries there is no such moment of empirical reflection,
at least in recent years, and the territorial differences are mostly
those collected within the single countries or by attempting *a
posteriori* comparisons.

Youth and Work: Between Continuity and Change

The elements of empirical knowledge here referred to do not
confirm the hypothesis of a deep change in youth's work value
orientations such as to foreshadow a solution of continuity with
the past. The relationship youth-work seems rather to place itself
in an evolutionary process, best expressed as follows: 'Youth and
work: between continuity and change'. Certainly the nonlinear
nature of the path demonstrates the difficulties in detailing factors
of change and the sub-groups of young people concerned, and it
excludes in itself the possibility of a final and global statement.
But the change, which certainly exists, is towards a strengthening
of the tendencies already present in the previous generation and a
harbinger of those that will be the general lines of tomorrow's
population.

In other words, rather than a widening gap there could well be
a kind of coming together and homogenisation of the population, a
process where, as far as the work ethic is concerned, youth are in
the vanguard, expanding on new values, attitudes and behaviour
that are not completely extraneous to other age groups.

If one considers only youth, however, the main conclusion is
once more: change in continuity. For example, the position of
refusing to work does not emerge from the empirical
investigations as a result, although people discussed it for a long
time in the 1970s and assumed it, at least in West European
countries, to be a specific characteristic of youth. What has

emerged, instead, is a kind of 'red line' which passes through all the national situations and the two socio-political systems involved: work appears as one of the activities, through which the young imbue their existence with meaning.

Youth - but not they alone - have an unemotional rational attitude which leads to seeking a job which permits them to express creativity and self-realisation as well as to have social relationships. These are aspirations that are found also in the subgroups most badly hit by unemployment - where attention to job security and stability, or even the critical acceptance of any job, influences the way work is experienced and perceived.

Such general statements about youth's work value orientations - which play an important role within the process of transition from school to work - therefore have always to be limited to specific social and time contexts. Up to now, they have not been in a position to provide sufficient reasons and insights to answer a large scope of important questions which need further inquiry more precisely. Among these is the nature of the current phase of economic and social development: Is there or is there not an epochal change passing from the industrial society to a different one (post-industrial or whatever defined)? It is not possible to solve this problem making use of old theoretical and methodological outlines capable of explaining the past but not the present. Is it therefore necessary to continue to investigate such questions as: What is the present youth's value orientation; is it different from what it has been; which are the leading values of the time; what are the effects of the increasingly more widespread technological and organisational changes on work ethics; what is work today and who constitute the class of 'youth' today? Such questions are not new; they are recurrently answered from different ideological points of view, with reference to general and specific problems and also with respect to the youth-work relationship (Baethge, 1985; Roberts, 1985; Pearl, 1985).

But this is just one more reason to continue the search for a better answer. The international project 'Transition of Young People from School to Work' is an effort to stimulate research and dialogue, from different philosophical and sociological perspectives, on this actual topic. As pointed out at the first meeting in Moscow - values (work values included) are among the main components of this complex problem. While attempting to focus research interest on some common issues of this problem and to use already existing theoretical and methodological premises and tools as much as possible - this project calls for an *open answer* - one which should be permanently under scrutiny for new methodologies and itself constantly questioning the truth of its own assertions.

That is the main reason why this chapter analysed not only some of the conclusions from the empirical data on the role of value change in youth's transition from school to work, but also focused on the *relationship between the empirical data* and *reality itself* and on the *theoretical and methodological models* used. Although the proposed interdisciplinary, mainly socio-psychological approach (exogenous/endogenous) and the frame of the three levels: macro-meso-micro of the social impact on individuals (and of their reciprocal action) - were substantiated by the empirical evidence, a substantial amount of theoretical and methodological shortcomings were also present. Among them were the difficulties (already mentioned) of defining and 'measuring' values in general and work values in particular; also, of analyzing the continuity versus change in youth's value orientation. Problems such as that of the 'anticipatory socialisation' nature of the changes in value orientation within the transition from school to work remained, however, unanswered.

New and better research projects are needed to improve on the present one; the main purpose of such an effort is not only scientific achievement as such, but even more so an understanding of the possible and necessary outcomes which can be achieved, for political policies for youth.

5

The Role of Education

Jo Diederen, Achim Hoffmann,
Peter Molnar and Michael Stefanov

Introduction

There is no doubt that the educational system affects the chances
and choices of individuals when they enter the labour market. But
it is not always clear how it does so. In the different
socioeconomic systems and even within the various countries, the
form and content of education differs sharply - the natural
outcome of the specific economic, political and cultural
development of a given nation. The comparative analysis of
educational systems is a matter too complicated for this study. In
this chapter, therefore, neither existing educational systems nor
their efficiency with respect to the process of transition from
school to work is evaluated. Attention is focused instead on
questions of a more general character: What is, at present and in
different countries, the role of education in determining social
opportunity; does education mitigate the role played by social
background; and, what are the requirements of an educational
system from this point of view?

These three questions coincide and complement each other to
such an extent that only as a unit do they create a true picture of
the role of education in the transition from school to work. Even
so, the picture is only a partial one. The focus on the educational
system causes the role played by other institutions such as the
labour market and the employment system itself to be deliberately
excluded. These aspects are dealt with in other chapters.

The task is complicated because each educational system has
its specific national characteristics which have been developed by
historical traditions and a unique socioeconomic development.
That is why, in dealing with this topic, national peculiarities and

experience form the starting point. This approach has two obvious advantages: first, it allows some terminological discrepancies to be avoided, while still offering a common ground for an interpretation of the different phenomena to be found; and second, a presentation of national situations gives some possibilities of understanding the achievements as well as the basic problems of the various educational cultures.

The educational system has numerous roles in each system of social relations. In connection with the process of the transition to work, the most important ones are the qualifying and selecting (or allocating) functions.[1] This refers to how the educational system selects people for certain types and levels of education, and how these people are then prepared for different social positions in society. The fundamental connection between the spheres of education and of production is reflected in these functions.

At least two steps can be specified in the transition process. The first is the moment of entering the different subdivisions of the educational system, where factors such as social background, individual abilities, interests and value system play their roles; the second is the moment of entering the sphere of production, where the main factor is the professional qualification of the individual, such as that achieved in the educational system.

The situation in Bulgaria, the German Democratic Republic, Hungary and the Netherlands is described here. Some of the remarkable differences and similarities between these countries with respect to the role played by education are pointed out in the conclusion.

Bulgaria

Structure of Education

Basic and primary education encompasses the age group from 6 to 15, i.e. from the 1st to the 8th class in schools of general education, and is compulsory. After basic education, two routes are open: Secondary general education aims at providing young people with a broader general preparation and cultural background in view of their orientation to higher education.

The introduction of polytechnical elements in secondary general education contributes to providing young people with a certain vocational training as well. Secondary professional edu-

Table 5.1: Some basic characteristics of the Bulgarian Educational System

	Index	1960 Total	1960 %	1970 Total	1970 % to 1960	1975 Total	1975 % to 1960	1980 Total	1980 % to 1960	1982 Total	1982 % to 1960
Pre-School Education	1	303	100	368	121.4	442	145.9	483	159.4	466	153.8
	2	32.9	100	40.9	124.3	46.7	141.9	50.8	154.4	52.4	159.3
Secondary General Education (1-11 grade)	3	1 213	100	1 157	95.4	1 102	90.1	1 096	90.3	1 174	96.8
	4	51.3	100	54.5	106.2	56.7	110.5	59.8	116.6	69.5	135.5
	5	5 884	100	4 206	71.5	3 760	63.9	3 590	61.0	3 556	60.4
	6	206.1	100	275.1	133.5	293.1	142.2	305.3	148.1	330.1	160.2
	7	24		21		19		18		17	
Secondary vocational education — Secondary	8	42.1	100	130	308.8	146	346.8	151	358.7	124	294.5
Vocational	9	236	100	328	139.0	315	133.8	300	127.1	284	120.3
Technical	10	96.9	100	159	164.1	153	157.9	107	110.4	102	105.3
Colleges	11	5.3	100	9.1	171.7	10.2	192.4	9.7	183.0	9.3	175.5
	12	236	100	256	108.5	258	109.3	242	102.5	237	100.4
	13	13.0	100	36.2	282.3	47.3	363.8	33.4	256.9	29.5	226.9
Higher Education	14	55.0	100	91.6	166.5	111.0	201.8	87.2	158.5	85.2	154.9
	15	3.2	100	5.5	171.9	9.7	303.1	10.7	334.4	13.3	415.6
	16	26.0	100	27.0	103.8	27.0	103.8	31.0	119.2	32.0	123.1
	17	5.8	100	13.1	225.9	15.4	265.5	20.0	344.8	17.0	293.1

Index: see next page.

Index
1. Total number of children (in thousands)
2. Relative proportion of children of pre-school age encompassed in pre-school education
3. Number of students in the full course of the general schools (in thousands)
4. Number of teachers (in thousands)
5. Number of schools
6. Average number of students in one school
7. Average number of students to one teacher
8. Number of students (in thousands)
9. Number of schools
10. Number of students (in thousands)
11. Number of teachers (in thousands)
12. Number of schools
13. Completed technical colleges (in thousands)
14. Number of students (in thousands)
15. Number of teachers (in thousands)
16. Number of higher educational institutions
17. Number of people graduating from higher ed. institutions (in thousands)

Source: *CMEA Statistical Yearbook*, 1983, pp. 400-10.

cation is accomplished through professional-technical schools, secondary professional-technical schools and technical colleges. Industrial-technical schools enroll young people after they have completed their primary education, and the duration varies from 2 to 3 years. These schools provide students with a general education and train them for certain jobs. A visible decline in the number of students wishing to attend such schools has been registered, which is primarily to be attributed to higher educational aspirations on the part of young people. In the 1970s, secondary professional schools and technical colleges attracted a growing number of young people. In the 1980s, there is evidence of a general decline in the number of students, but nevertheless the number of applicants is still much higher than these schools can absorb.

The system of higher education also reflects the societal needs during the present stage of the country's socioeconomic development. Whereas there was a sharp increase in the number of university students in the 1970s, we have witnessed a rise in the number of university teachers in the 1980s. This naturally leads to a further intensification of the process of education (see Table 5.1).

The New Educational System

The demand to create favourable social conditions for young
people to take part in production is the underlying principle of the
educational reform that was implemented at the beginning of the
1980s.

The basic educational unit in the new educational system is
now the *unified secondary polytechnic school* (USPS). At the
first level, which lasts ten years, teaching now commences at the
age of six and not at seven as was the case before. Education, at
this level, is aimed at providing extensive general schooling;
forming habits and lasting motives for work; developing cognitive
skills; and at revealing and fostering aptitudes, talents and creative
aspirations.

The *educational-professional complex* is the organisational
form of training at the second and third levels of the USPS. Up to
three years of training takes place, depending on the requirements
of the respective professional sector and is based on uniform
mandatory norms of general education and general-technical
instruction. A certain differentiation and flexibility is introduced,
however, allowing some students to finish school in a shorter
period of time. As an exception, some of those completing the first
level - depending on their wishes and on the character of the
respective occupation - obtain certain qualifications without
having to attend the second and third levels, and pass directly into
the sphere of production and services. Conditions have been
created for these young people to eventually complete their
secondary education in the form of evening courses or education
without leaving the job. At the second and third levels, students
are involved in production for certain periods of time and given
the status of student-probationer (student-worker).

The necessity for further improvement in higher education and
a decisive increase in the quality of the educational process have
led to certain amendments in Bulgaria's system of *higher
education* as well. Three levels also exist here. The first level
provides fundamental, general theoretical schooling in a certain
professional field; the second level ensures the orientation and
training of the specialist for a profession with a broad profile; and
the third level furnishes specialisation in production itself or in
research activities and intends to offer high professional
qualifications in a narrow, specialised field. The duration of
studies at these three levels is flexible and differentiated, the

general term of education varying from 4 to 6 years. Professional specialisation, which to a great extent determines how the transition from school to work takes place, is carried out at the enterprises to which the student has been directed at the end of the second level of education. In cases where these enterprises lack the possibilities of ensuring specialisation in the profession studied, students are directed to other enterprises or to special educational facilities.

Social Background, Work, and Work Content

The findings of sociological surveys carried out at different stages in the development of the system of education indicate that the introduction of the new educational system in Bulgaria has a positive effect on the transition from school to work.

The quality of young people's vocational training has definitely been improved. Whereas in 1977, 30% to 40% of the students completing secondary special education and 60% of those completing general education gave the vocational training they received at school a very low rating;[2] in the late 1980s 80% to 90% of those in this category were of the opinion that they had received very good and excellent theoretical and practical training. Research findings show that some 60% of all young people can be incorporated directly into the production process of an enterprise in which they have worked as probationers, and that a mere 9% are not able to cope with the tasks imposed on them in a working situation.

Positive changes are also evident in regard to the desire of individuals to practice and work in their area of specialisation after their secondary education has been completed. Obviously, the type of secondary education needs to be taken into account here. Among students from technical schools and secondary professional schools, high levels of orientation to work in the studied specialisation (around 70%) seems to be quite natural. After the Education Production Complexes were founded, the number of those wishing to work in their area of specialisation doubled - even in general educational schools (26% compared to 13% in the 1970s). At the same time, however, in this type of school young people who prefer another occupation, either one close to their area of specialisation or one entirely different from it, are in the the majority. In the light of an analysis of the process of transition from school to work, this brings the issue of the realisation of an initial professional orientation as a condition for a successful transition from education to the sphere of work to the foreground. This is also one of the most important problems confronting the transition from the system of higher education to work.

Table 5.2: Workers and employees younger and older than 30 years by educational level (as per December 31, 1984)*

Educational level	Numbers				Percentage		
	Total	Up to 30 years	Over 30 years	Total	Up to 30 years	Over 30 years	% of youths in each group
Higher	322 277	61 481	260 796	7.8	7.6	7.9	19.6
Semi-higher	145 358	35 955	109 403	3.5	4.5	3.3	19.0
Secondary special	594 527	184 407	405 120	14.5	23.5	12.3	24.7
Secondary general	823 498	260 337	563 161	20.1	32.3	17.1	31.9
Primary and lower	2 220 715	259 131	1 961 584	54.1	32.1	59.4	31.6
Total	4 106 375	806 311	3 300 064	100.0	100.0	100.0	10.6

*According to data of the Committee for a Unified System of Social Information with the Council of Ministers of the People's Republic of Bulgaria.

A strong factor in determining the transition from school to work is the parental family with its specific climate, traditions and objective social position. As for the educational level of Bulgaria's working youth in general, it can be said that the educational level of the younger generation is higher than that of the adult generation. This conclusion is substantiated both by the analysis of general statistical data (see Table 5.2) and by sociological studies dealing with the relation between the educational level of young people and that of their parents (see Table 5.3). While it is the case that this study has focused on young manual workers and their parents, the general tendencies also apply to other groups of working youth.

Table 5.3: Levels of education, young Bulgarians and their parents (%)

	Fathers	Mothers	Young people
Lower than incomplete secondary	55.3	60.0	1.9
Incomplete secondary	16.5	15.7	14.3
Vocational technical without secondary	5.1	4.5	6.7
Secondary general	8.7	11.4	14.8
Vocational technical with secondary	-	-	18.7
Technical college	6.0	4.2	35.2
Semi-higher education	3.0	2.8	0.9
Higher education	5.4	1.5	7.5

Data from Mitev *et al.* 'Life Paths of Working Youth in the Socialist Countries', 1983a.

There are differences in the family influence which can be attributed to the educational level of parents. Thus, for instance, about 35% of Bulgarian students attending higher educational establishments come from families where the father has a higher education and 18% come from families where the mother has a higher education; 37% have fathers with secondary education and 50% have mothers with secondary education. In families where the parents have only a primary education, the respective figures are 25% versus 25%; and in families where the parents have only a basic education, it is 4% and 7%. The conclusion can be drawn, therefore, that the degree of realisation of a young person's initial professional orientation as a condition for a smooth transition to the sphere of work is inversely proportional to the educational level of the parents.[3]

A significant factor influencing the professional orientation of students is the type of secondary education they have had followed. In Bulgaria, 64% of all students in higher education have completed secondary general educational schools, 33% have completed technical colleges, and only 3% have completed vocational schools. Two correlations are to be clearly discerned: first, the lower the educational level on which the professional orientation is based, the higher is its stability; second, the various types of secondary education provide different opportunities for the realisation of the initial professional orientation of young people. Some 31% of all young workers do not work in the occupation they have been trained for. In lower age brackets, however, the lack of correspondence between job and training is not as high (about 25%). Nevertheless, the fact that one out of every four workers has sought another field of work does pose questions about the quality of vocational training, at least at the lower level. The basic problem in this respect concerns the achievements of a correspondence between preconceived ideas about the work characteristics of a given occupation and the reality of the job. Young people who start working in material production in the late 1980s have a rather vague idea about the job requirements and the conditions of work at their specific work place. The group of those where there is an incongruity between preconceived ideas and reality consists of 37% of young people aged 16 to 20 and 35% of those aged 21 to 25. The analysis of the influence of the various types of educational establishments on the formation of adequate ideas in a young person about the peculiarities of a specific occupation leads to the conclusion that the transition from education to work through the system of vocational training offers slightly better chances for a smooth transition (See Table 5.4).

Table 5.4: Professional qualification structure of young Bulgarians (aged 16-29) with differing levels of education (%)

Completed education	Professional-qualificational status of young people on entry into first job						
	A	B	C	D	E	F	G
Lower than secondary	71.8	28.2	0.0	-	-	-	100.0
Secondary general	7.2	55.7	13.6	11.6	10.5	0.8	100.0
Secondary vocational-technical	18.4	59.2	9.5	4.2	8.7	0.0	100.0

A=Unqualified workers, B=Medium qualified workers, C=Highly qualified workers, D=Unqualified employees, E=Medium qualified employees, F=Highly qualified employees, G=Total

Source: P.E. Mitev *et al.*, *Youth and Labour*, 1983a, p. 293.

A more detailed analysis reveals the following picture:

- youth entering work after completing their primary or

secondary general education show, relatively often, a complete lack of correspondence between their professional image and professional reality;
- youth entering the work force after completing their vocational-technical, secondary vocational-technical or secondary-special school show, relatively often, at least a partial correspondence between professional image and professional reality;
- youth entering the world of work after completing their vocational-technical or secondary-general education most often do not practice the profession they were trained for.

A definite idea about the intensity and the factors influencing work mobility can be obtained by reviewing the reasons why jobs are changed. As a rule, youth (especially up to the age of 20) is less involved in mobility than the older generations. It we look at the role of training, received prior to entering the working world this phenomenon is observed most frequently among those young people who start work immediately after completing their primary education or vocational-technical school (i.e. the lowest degree of vocational training). At the same time, those who interrupt their participation in the work process in order to achieve degrees of higher education tend to be young people with a low level of education who then attend secondary vocational schools, secondary special schools or higher educational institutions.

A definite range of problems characterizing the quality of the transition from education to work refers to the difficulties that a young person experiences most frequently when looking for his first job. The significance of these problems is highlighted by the statistic that only about 41% of all young workers have not met with serious difficulties while seeking employment for the first time.

The following picture emerges when rating the difficulties: insufficient practical knowledge and skills are the basic reasons leading to problems among 35% of all young workers; working conditions cause difficulties for 16%; working with unfamiliar equipment affects 16%; insufficient expertise is a factor for 16%; problems with the work collective is a problem for 15% and the fulfilment of production quality quotas causes difficulties for 10%.

The analysis of the causes underlying young workers' change of jobs and their retraining are important for an understanding of the transition process. However, the issue of how typical such phenomena are for the period of transition is controversial since occupations are also changed in later stages of one's working life. Nevertheless, young people aged 21 to 25 are in the majority of those who change their job owing to: the lack of appropriate work corresponding to one's area of specialisation (39%), monotonous work (35%), better opportunities for professional growth by taking a new occupation (35%), inability to achieve harmony with the work collective (40%).

One can distinguish between social and personal opportunities for young people to develop professional careers. Social opportunities are defined by the possibilities offered by society (number and type of educational establishments and available places, number and types of jobs, etc.). In this case, the needs for qualified workers in the different spheres of social production act as a regulating mechanism. Personal opportunities are defined by the ability of the personality to meet social requirements. Naturally, there are certain limits to the possibilities for satisfying needs, and these too are reflected in the educational system.

In Bulgaria, the system of secondary education as a whole is set up in such a way that it can absorb all the young people who want to raise their level of education. Those limitations having a social character are to be found in the inner structure and content of the educational system which reflects societal needs for workers with definite training. The limitations of a personal character are to be found in the inability or unwillingness of young people to enter a secondary educational establishment.

The situation in the system of higher education is quite similar. There the societal needs for a certain number of specialists with the highest level of qualifications are lower in comparison to the societal needs for specialists with a medium level of qualifications; this logically leads to a strict monitoring of numbers of students to be admitted, and therefore to more strict requirements in respect to personal qualities. In contemporary Bulgaria, a young person is not faced with the issue of whether he will find employment or not. The basic issue that concerns him in the 1980s is the type of work he shall find.

The German Democratic Republic

The Educational System

The educational system determines the preconditions with which an individual begins his working life. While, in 1971, about 61% of all working people had completed the training for a vocation (among them 4% who had graduated from university and 7% who had finished technical and engineering schools), their number had increased to over 83% by 1983 (with 7% university graduates and over 13% being graduates from technical and engineering schools). As a consequence, the entrance of ever better educated young people into the working process has become a typical phenomenon. The general polytechnical comprehensive school (which has 10 years of education) provides its pupils with a modern, socialist, general education as a basis for further studies. This applies to approximately 80% of all school-graduates who either undergo vocational training to become qualified skilled workers or who graduate from secondary school (2 to 3 additional years) with a general certificate of education for study at an institution of higher education. On the average, about 25% of all pupils of the same age have higher levels of education, that is to say, they have graduated from a university or have completed a technical school.[4]

Apart from this route, there are various other forms and institutions of special education which take particular abilities, interests and talents into account (such as children's and young people's sport schools, schools with extended language classes and schools or classes specialising in mathematics and physics). A further development of the content and structure of the educational system aims at satisfying the different demands for job qualification while, *at the same time*, guaranteeing the growing need for creative and innovative work performance. A concept of general education, which will be basically reasonable and valid over a long period, is needed to assure an efficient transition from school to work. The central aim here is to realise an efficient shaping of personalities in the educational process, so that young people will be able, and ready, to take part in radical changes resulting from social development.

To achieve this purpose, the following subjects are taught at the general polytechnical comprehensive school:

- the social sciences and the German language 41.1%
- maths/natural sciences 29.8%
- introduction into production/productive work 10.6%
- foreign languages 10.6%
- sports 7.9%

Together, mathematics and German account for about 45% of all classes. Thus, they represent the largest proportion of courses devoted to general education.

Research findings show that young people with a high level of general education and those who are better qualified are not only more adequately prepared for their jobs than those with a low level of general education but also often achieve their job aspirations. The lower an individual's general education is, the less concrete are his job expectations and a career is less likely to be the centre of his orientation towards life.

More qualified young people have specific ideas about work: variation on the job, a working collective which functions well and an independent field of work rank highest among their desires for future employment. Research indicates that persons with early job orientation, those who make efforts to enter the desired job through excellent performance and the level of a person's general education have a large impact on an efficient transition from school to work. It should be noted that the polytechnical comprehensive school is to lay the foundation for an all-round and harmonic personality development. This means that it is not intended to be a preacademic educational institution. Over 80% of all school-graduates take up vocational training and accept jobs as skilled workers. From the point of view of the growing need for life-long learning, a general education must also guarantee that young people develop the interests, abilities, and value orientations to continue to develop themselves.

Polytechnical education seems to offer a particularly favourable starting point for an efficient transition from school to work which requires, under 1980s conditions, an integration of work education in the entire process of education and the laying of a solid foundation for the vocational training and flexibility of the future worker. The positive effects of this concept are evident in the relatively high satisfaction young people have with the occupation they have trained for and in a relatively low job fluctuation situation over the first five years of their employment. At the same time, however, research findings suggest that many young people (including students) enter working life with excessive and, in part, inadequate expectations.

Table 5.5: Selected aspirations of the German Democratic Republic youth about their work in the next 5 to 10 years (%)

| | Apprenticeship | | Employment | |
	1st Year	2nd Year	1st Year	2nd Year
Variation at the job	94	93	93	96
An independent field of work	93	93	95	95
Learning new things	95	92	93	92
Being well paid	91	91	90	87
Working in a collective which functions well	91	89	91	92
Opportunities for one's vocational development	95	88	87	83
Challenging work	64	57	69	67
Social respect of the job	54	50	48	46
A clean job	55	38	36	41
Little efforts	-	18	14	13

Source: W. Friedrich and H. Müller, *Zur Psychologie der 12 bis 22 jährigen*, 1980, p. 232.

As vocational training continues and concrete job and in-plant experiences grow, the ideals entertained by youth gradually become more realistic. But the data from Table 5.5 also illustrate the relative stability and balance of basic expectations, in some cases even against real experience. Implementing the principle of polytechnical education is not a specific or additional task, but an essential aspect of education.

- the organisation of productive work for pupils of different ages and pupils following different courses of education;
- opportunities to introduce theoretical issues of production into the curricula;
- the opportunity for pupils to do practical work in science;
- the confrontation between social everyday experiences and theoretical knowledge during the education process;
- the development of both individual responsibility and collective responsibility by pupils for production-related tasks when doing practical work;

- a continuous modernisation of specialised courses which include advances in science, technology and production;
- to use the potential inherent in specialised education to educate attitudes towards work.

The intention to have students make their choice for further education after the seventh grade (which is done now after the ninth grade) will further create favourable conditions for a closer bond between school and life. The experiences made in solving complex tasks (which are modeled along those to be found on the actual job market and the high degree of independent intellectual activity which is needed to accomplish this promote independence, creativity, flexibility and a collective consciousness.

The Impact of Social Background

In general, social background has largely lost its traditional function of determining social position, educational level, and job efficiency. All children have, independent of their social background, the same opportunities for education in the general polytechnical comprehensive school, for additional vocational training, and for getting a job. Also, discrimination against women both in the field of education and when it comes to qualifications has largely been overcome.

Nevertheless, research confirms that when parents have a predominantly intellectual and creative job, more favourable conditions are created to meet their children's demands for education and employment. The higher the educational level of the parents, the more specific are their children's expectations in regard to education. Children of highly qualified parents have socially determined advantages that serve to reinforce their motivations given that these motivations are accompanied by adequate positive ratings at school. Hence, these children often do particularly well in school and are more likely to aim for an educational institution which offers them matriculation in order to qualify for intellectual and creative job opportunities later in life. Thus, basic personal life orientations of young people are essentially determined by their family background. However, the dividing line is mainly found between youth from parents who lack qualifications altogether or whose parents have low qualifications and children from skilled workers or parents with higher qualifications (differences between children from the last two groups are negligible, see Table 5.6).

Table 5.6: Work expectations in the 1st year of apprenticeship related to the occupational qualification of the father (%) (only positive extreme value = 'very important')

Father	Integration into the work collective	Independent work	Varied work	Creative demands	Career opportunities
No qualifications/partially skilled worker	47	34	47	6	32
Skilled worker	42	42	55	11	38
Graduate from a technical engineering school	44	48	57	17	43
Graduate from university or college	52	38	58	12	41

Source: W. Friedrich and H. Müller, *Zur Psychologie der 12 bis 22 jährigen*, 1980, p. 207.

Income and even social background, have clearly lost their significance as differentiating factors. The qualification level of one's parents has become the main criterion for young people's decisions concerning the job they aim for: those who come from highly qualified families tend to be oriented towards a given career and a given educational path at an earlier age than those whose families have lower qualifications; they make their choices sooner and with more motivation and greater stability than young persons from families with a low level of qualifications.

This is also why the stimulation and encouragement of children from families with blue-collar and monotonous jobs still pose many problems. Efforts among these social groups are increasingly being directed towards stimulating occupational, intellectual and cultural interests as well as motivation for education and a desire for knowledge.

Basic Problems and Intended Solutions

Problems concerning a lack of coordination between the qualifications and the aspirations of young people and the real employment situation facing them in the outside world cannot, in this general form, be confirmed for the German Democratic Republic. However, the fundamental problems which are known to need solutions are:

- An efficient use by society of the achieved level of qualification. Education related to work-practice and life, continuing education and, in particular, retraining need to gain in value. This requires more flexible training and employment strategies.
- The maintenance of a level of employment which corresponds to qualifications and educational levels in order to avoid overqualification on the job.
- The use of youth's flexibility as a stimulating factor for the national economy (young people have to be systematically prepared to be able to master innovation processes).
- The various forms of youth organisations (youth brigades, youth projects, youth research collectives, etc.) which, apart from their economic significance, should also have an important function in integrating young people into work and work collectives.
- Long-term attitudes which stimulate life-long qualifications, relearning and necessary job changes - thus increasing the mobility of youth, need to be formed at an even earlier age than has been the case so far.

In the German Democratic Republic, it is argued that the main solutions are not to be found in an improvement of the qualifications attained during the original training period or in a prolongation of the time spent being educated but in the very concept of education primarily, in a specific extension of general education, in a closer relationship between school and life (by consistently applying the polytechnical principle) and in a meaningful co-ordination between the activities of youth organisations and the job-preparing tasks of the school system.

Hungary

Structure of Education

Basic, compulsory education starts in Hungary at the age of six and lasts for 10 years. Primary school takes eight years and is divided into a lower and an upper section. The lower section is taught by one teacher for each year of school while in the upper section, the instruction is carried out by different teachers, who each specialise in one subject, for each class. The opportunity to have a secondary school education has more or less followed demand of society. As a consequence, these opportunities have been lower than the number of youth interested when the youth made up a large group, especially in the case of secondary general education. After finishing primary school, some 48% of the children go on to attend vocational training schools. This did not change much between 1978 and 1983. Those enrolled in the vocational secondary school numbered 24% at the beginning and 27% at the end of the same period. The situation at grammar schools has not changed significantly either (20%-21%).

Table 5.7: Educational level of Hungarian youth at the time of the first job (%)

	1974[1]	1978[2]	1980	1983
University, college	8.3	6.5	12.3	11.1
Grammar school	8.0	9.2	6.1	6.5
Vocational secondary school	11.8	17.9	15.3	16.2
Apprentice training school	38.6	30.5	37.8	35.7
Primary school graduates	23.6	29.4	23.6	25.8
Primary school dropouts	9.7	6.5	4.9	4.7

Source:
[1]Hungarian Statistical Yearbook, 1984.
[2]T. Erdész and P. Molnár, 'A fiatalok iskolázottsága pályakezdésük idején' (Utilisation of Education at the Professional Start), *Munkaügyi Szemle*, 1986.

The vocational training school does not include a secondary school qualification; however, it enables young skilled workers to start a technical secondary study at an evening school or through correspondence courses. The majority of the professions learned at the vocational training school require three years of education. Grammar school has a double function: preparation for university and college studies and seeing that the young have a smooth adjustment to practical life when looking for employment. Over the years, its task of preparing young people for further studies has been strengthened, but the question as to how to give sufficient preparation to those who do not continue their studies has not been solved yet. Vocational secondary school concentrates on general and overall theoretical and practical training which is comprised of several related branches.

The final examination prepares the pupil for immediate employment in his area of specialisation. It also allows him to apply for further study at any university or college. The structure of the secondary school system is, however, rather inflexible; it also has a relatively narrow scope when it comes to the teaching of easily convertible, basic knowledge, and it concentrates too early on specialised expert knowledge.

A relatively large number of young people begin working with only a general school certification or even without having completed primary school: this is the case for some 30% to 35% of every young generation (see Table 5.7).

The Hungarian School Reform

The main result of the development of public education was a general increase in the level of schooling in the last decade. The number of children attending nursery school increased to 91% in 1981. The school education of pupils aged 6-16 after 1980 is virtually complete (98%); in the 1980s 95% of all school children successfully complete primary school by the age of 16 and 93% of them continue their studies at the secondary school level. The increase in the possibilities for schooling have affected all the classes and strata of society; it has also further reduced uneven levels of education among them.

While important changes concerning the content of the educational process have taken place, a number of negative characteristics still burden the educational system. Grammar schools and vocational schools are still not well enough co-ordinated with each other, vocational training as such is not particularly well-adjusted to the present needs of the employment system or to its future needs and the actual structure of secondary school education is too narrowly streamlined, leaving only a few choices to pursue at the university level.

Social Mobility

There is a radical change in social relations characterising the structure of society as a whole. In the course of the last one and a half decades, the class-based differences have been increasingly reduced.

There has been a very high rate of mobility between the generations as well as within the generations, especially during the first years of employment. The basis for our analysis of mobility patterns is the proportion of young people who started working in a group different from that of their parents. We have to distinguish between 'added' and 'returning' mobility. In the case of added mobility, young people start at the same type of job that their parents had but later leave it. In the case of returning mobility, young people whose first job was not in the occupational group of their parents return to this occupational group later. It can be said that these two types of mobility are numerically balanced, i.e. the extent of general intergeneration mobility is not significantly affected by it.

Table 5.8: Development of inter-generational and intra-generational mobility in the Hungarian industry (%)

Father's social group	Ratio of the mobile young at the time of the first job	Added mobility	Returning mobility	Inter-generational mobility
Unskilled worker	69	15	-	84
Semi-skilled worker	91	-	20	71
Skilled worker	55	8	-	63
White-collar worker without special education	87	-	4	83
White-collar worker with special education	84	-	8	76
Intellectual worker	84	-	8	76
Total	69	1	-	70

Source: P. Mitev *et al., Youth and Labour*, Sofia, 1983, p. 251.

Detailed data show that intergeneration mobility, at 69%, is still very high.[5] Added mobility is especially important for the unskilled workers - it is associated with higher qualifications and less-strenuous physical labour. Returning mobility is also high because of the extension of education on higher levels through

Table 5. 9: Educational level of Hungarian youth when first employed compared to the occupational status of the father (in 1978) (%)

Educational level of youth	A	B	C	D	E	F	G
Employee with higher educational level and in leading position	16.8	16.0	26.5	22.1	18.6	0.0	100 (7.2)
Employee graduated from technical colleges, vocational technical school, etc.	15.5	15.5	32.8	25.9	10.3	0.0	100 (3.7)
Employee without special training	11.9	21.4	26.2	21.4	16.7	2.4	100 (5.3)
Skilled worker	4.7	9.3	21.0	31.8	27.8	5.2	100 (42.7)
Semiskilled worker and unskilled worker	3.6	6.3	10.4	35.9	35.1	8.8	100 (23.2)
Unskilled worker in agriculture	6.5	6.1	10.2	29.8	38.4	9.0	100 (15.6)
Artisan, independent retailer	5.7	22.9	25.7	14.3	17.1	14.3	100
Total	6.5	9.8	18.1	30.6	29.0	6.1	100

A=University college, B=Grammar school, C=Vocational secondary school, D=Apprentice training school, E=Completed compulsory school, F=Uncompleted compulsory school, G=Total
(3 categories) Pearson's R=0.259

Source: F. Gazsó et al., *Pályakezdők az iparban* (Professional Start in Industry), 1984.

evening classes, which is mainly utilised by the children of white-collar workers. In contrast to this, opportunities offered by

Hungarian training schools for skilled workers are not adequately made use of: as is proven by the 20% returning mobility statistic of young people who are the children of semi-skilled families. The main reason for this is that wages for some semi-skilled jobs are relatively high. This is also the reason for a high dropout rate in secondary education. (See Table 5.8).

In Hungary, the educational system has a decisive influence on mobility as an intermediate factor. First, the social background of the family influence the level and type of studies a young person pursues in the educational system; secondly, the educational system has a decisive influence on the first job a youth gets and on the social status he receives at the beginning of his working life. Tables 5.9 and 5.10 show that the correlation in the latter case is significantly higher (0.67) than in the first one (0.26). Although a lower educational level does not exclude the possibility of intergenerational mobility, the chance is very limited. Of all young people having finished eight classes 65% are working as unskilled

Table 5.10: Occupational status of Hungarian youth by educational level when first employed

	A	B	C	D	E	F	
University/college	84.7	14.4	0.0	0.9	0.0	100	(6.3)
Grammar school	5.2	38.7	22.0	22.5	11.5	100	(9.7)
Vocational secondary school	9.1	50.9	6.3	29.7	4.0	100	(17.9)
Apprentice training school	0.4	10.1	3.8	73.7	11.9	100	(30.9)
Primary school graduates	0.2	6.2	16.4	12.2	65.0	100	(29.0)
Primary school dropouts	0.0	0.0	4.5	3.6	91.9	100	(6.2)
Total	7.6	18.7	9.5	34.1	30.1	100	

A=Intellectual worker, B=White-collar worker with special education, C=White-collar worker without special education, D=Skilled worker, E=Unskilled worker, semi-skilled worker, F=Total
International comparison (3 categories) Pearson's R=0.673

Source: F. Gazsó *et al.*, *Pályakezdők az iparban* (Professional Start in Industry), 1984.

workers. The mobility possibilities of those who graduated in skilled-workers schools, without having achieved the final examination certificate, are also very restricted. Favourable chances for intergeneration mobility are linked to secondary general school attendance. Nevertheless, schooling still has a high subjective significance, as proved by Hungarian data according to which 18% of the young people reached a higher qualification while performing their regular occupational work.

In spite of the fact, that there are broad possibilities for those who want to continue their studies while working, these have no essential influence on the basic function of the regular school system. It is fully valid even today, that the school-system is a prominent agent for the reproduction of social inequality and for the regulation of social mobility. Indications for this are presented by the existence of some typical careers so, for instance, the skilled worker training of the less successful pupils in the lower grades; the high percentage of girls in some of the secondary schools, and later in some specific branches; the high degrees of young people in some jobs where high wages are paid but which are fully irrelevant for the country's economic development; and the deterioration of efficiency and prestige associated with advanced technical studies at the university level.

Overall, chances for finding employment continue to be relatively promising. In educational policy circles, it has been recognised that the problems of young people will become increasingly serious if the exigencies for achieving degrees in higher education and special qualifications are not enhanced and their application is not stressed more than is the case in the 1980s. For this reason, the content of specialist training needs to be modernised so that graduates will meet the economic-technical requirements of the enterprises where - after all - youth is bound to find employment. At the same time, young people are to get a broader general education which they are to be able to draw on at more than one specific working place. In Hungary, this new policy is mostly oriented at a comprehensive type of school where general education, combined with training, develops the skills young people need for the future. Preparing the young for standing on their own in the social division of labour is the main task of this comprehensive type school. It is most likely that, in the 1980s, the close connection between formal school education and occupational status will be loosened - at least during the first years after leaving school. Continuing special training in line with the evolution in technology and actual problems will take over a major role in educating populations.

The Netherlands

The Structure of the Educational System

The Dutch educational system has three levels: primary, secondary and higher education. Primary education is for four to twelve year-old pupils, secondary education is for pupils aged 12 to 18 or 19, and higher education is for the age group beyond this. Since the Compulsory Education Act of 1975, there is full-time compulsory education for those under 16 (ten years of required education) and partial compulsory education for 16 year-olds (two days a week). The formal structure of secondary education was established in the Mammoth Act of 1968. Some structural features will be emphasised here because these are essential for an adequate understanding of recent developments in the vocational component of the educational system. There are two clearly separated types of education after primary education: general education and vocational education. Both general and vocational education have a strong hierarchical structure. About 30% of those completing their primary education pursue their education at a (preparatory) vocational school. Their choice of vocation is determined at the age of 12 because the vocational education which follows at the secondary level is already divided into a number of strongly separated areas: technical education, domestic education, economic and business education, social-pedagogic education, and so on. General secondary education offers a relatively large number of possibilities for pupils to continue their education at other levels of general education as well as in the form of training in a vocation. As a result of the increasing participation in education over the past two decades, participation in lower general education (*MAVO*) after primary school has increased enormously. Although the *MAVO* still offers a complete course of study in itself for a large number of young people (about 10% of all pupils), a growing number of these continue their education at a higher level. As opposed to general education, vocational education is structurally limited when it comes to offering possibilities for pupils to continue full-time education; opportunities only appear at the next level of vocational education. In practice, however, vocational education appears to be the final education for most pupils, regardless of the level. The traditional target group for craftsmanship at the lower levels of the employment scale - those who have completed junior vocational education (*LBO*) - is offered only one opportunity for continuing education full-time: senior vocational education (*MBO*). Moreover, this is only open to those who have reached the highest level possible within the *LBO* system. The only other alternative until the 1980s was to follow the dual path of the apprenticeship system (working while attending school part-time. Altogether, about 75% enter the labour market after leaving the *LBO*.

The limited opportunities for additional education which are open to *LBO* graduates are known as the gap in the Mammoth. *LBO* and *MAVO* graduates enter the labour market without an initial vocational qualification: the *LBO* is preparatory vocational education and the *MAVO* is general education. About 250,000 graduates enter the Dutch labour market each year: 100,000 of these have attended the *LBO* (75,000) or the *MAVO* (25,000). Of this group, about one third has left school without receiving a certificate of graduation.

Since the late 1970s, the position of the *LBO* and the *MAVO* graduates on the apprenticeship and labour market has deteriorated. The unemployment rate, both in numbers and in duration, of this group of young people with the lowest level of education has increased substantially since the beginning of the 1980s; the number of apprenticeship positions, which are dependent on the conjunctural and structural developments in the labour market, has declined sharply. Labour market and educational policies have been confronted with absorption problems. At the same time, industry was expecting to confront difficulties in getting enough skilled craftsmen in the near future. It was pointing at the effect of technological and organisational developments in production processes, at the expected economic revival and at the expected 'greying' of its personnel. Moreover, skilled manpower was once again regarded as an essential condition for economic revival. Thus, not only was the absorption problem growing, but the demand for measures to provide industry with the qualified manpower needed in the near future became louder as well.

As a reaction to these two problems, the absorption problem and the (expected) qualification problem, policies have been developed to extend opportunities for vocational education/ training beyond that offered by the *LBO* and the *MAVO*. Unique to the Dutch situation is that, in 1983, the government, industry (employers and unions) and educational organisations discussed these problems and formulated new lines of policy ('Open

Consultations Wagner'). These parties have taken it upon themselves to jointly improve vocational education and to offer all young people the opportunity to acquire at least an initial vocational qualification. Usually this qualification is termed 'prospective craftsmanship' (Ministry of Education and Sciences, September 1984).

Social Background, Education and Occupation

Testing theories of social inequality was one of the aims of a longitudinal survey, begun in 1965, on the school and occupational careers of girls and boys who completed primary school that year.[6] The study had been set up to examine the relationship among social background, educational level and occupational level, and the results of this research are drawn on in the following analysis.

To indicate social background, the occupational level of the father in 1970 is used, in which year the 1965-cohort was about 17 years old. The following occupational levels are distinguished:

1	unskilled manual workers	10%
2	skilled manual workers	30%
3	farmers	10%
4	small entrepreneurs	13%
5	lower non-manual workers (employees)	20%
6	medium level employees	9%
7	higher occupations	8%

Table 5.11 shows that there is an evident correlation between social background, as indicated by occupational level of the father, and the education pursued by young people. When we compare the educational levels of children from different social classes the differences are striking. The higher the occupational level of the father

- the lower the percentage of children with incomplete vocational education;
- the lower the percentage of those with only lower level vocational education;
- the higher the percentage of those who attended grammar school;
- the higher the percentage of those with a medium level of

115

vocational education (although this trend is interrupted by a relatively high share of children from farmer families; these children have usually followed a medium level agrarian education);

-   the higher the percentage of children with a higher level of vocational education; and
-   the higher the percentage of children with a university level education.

Table 5.11: The educational level of the 1965-cohorts (rows) according to the occupational level of the father (columns) (%)

Occupational level of the father	1	2	3	4	5	6	7
Only primary education	6	5	1	1	3	1	
Continued primary education	1	5	2	4	2	1	
Vocational education without diploma	21	15	10	10	6	7	
General education without diploma	4	7	5	12	7	9	5
Lower vocational education	47	33	30	26	26	18	15
Intermediate general education	12	14	14	13	14	9	5
Secondary general or pre-university education	3	4	5	12	12	18	23
Intermediate vocational education	3	10	25	12	17	20	22
Higher vocational education	2	5	5	10	11	16	23
University			3	1	2	1	6
Total	100	100	100	100	100	100	100

1=unskilled worker, 2=skilled worker, 3=farmers, 4=small entrepreneurs, 5=lower manual workers (employees), 6=medium level employees, 7=higher occupations

A person's education, as we have seen, partly depends on the occupational level of the father, but is also an important determining factor of the occupational level a youth can attain. To measure the occupational level of the 1965-cohorts, it is necessary to look at the jobs they occupied at the ages of 22 - 25, and not at the first jobs they had after leaving the educational system. The reason for this is that the occupational level of youngsters in their first job is not comparable because each cohort left school at a different age, and so each has a different age when engaging in his first job. Moreover, the process of reaching a certain occupational level does not end with the first job: 73% of the 1965-cohorts changed their job before the age of 25, and 18% even changed their field of expertise in order to either improve their situation or to make it more in tune with their own interests. We may assume that this process has come to an end by the time the individuals have reached the ages of 22-25.

Table 5.12: The occupational level of individuals at the age of 22 - 25 (columns) according to their educational level (rows) (%)

Occupational level	1	2	3/4	5	6	7	0	total
Only primary education	35	43	2	17			2	100
Continued primary education	13	35	4	41	2	4		100
Vocational education without diploma	19	39	4	33	1	1	3	100
General education without diploma	4	21	6	57	8	1	3	100
Lower vocational education	9	45	2	35	5	1	2	100
Intermediate general education	2	9	3	72	10	4	1	100
Secondary general or preuniversity education	2	2	3	37	18	8	30	100
Intermediate vocational education	0	14	3	52	23	4	2	100
Higher vocational education	1	4		21	51	14	9	100
University				12	4	63	21	100

1=unskilled worker, 2=skilled worker, 3/4=farmers + small entrepreneurs, 5=lower manual workers (employees), 6=medium level employees, 7=higher occupations, 0=persons who had never worked

Table 5.12 shows the relationship between the educational

level and the occupational level reached. These relations suggest a number of definite transitional careers from school to work. Among them the most prominent appear to be:

- unskilled manual work after primary education and an uncompleted vocational education;
- skilled manual work after primary education and after completed or uncompleted lower vocational education;
- lower non-manual work after an uncompleted general education and after a general or vocational education at the intermediate level;
- non-manual work on a medium level after intermediate and higher vocational education;
- higher occupations after university studies;
- no job until the age of 25 after leaving compulsory education (persons still studying at a university).

Table 5.13: The occupational level of the 1965-cohorts (columns) according to social background as indicated by the occupational level of the father (rows) (%)

	1	2	3/4	5	6	7	0	total
1	15	40	3	34	6	1	2	100
2	11	32	1	40	10	3	3	100
3	5	27	10	37	12	4	4	100
4	5	19	6	46	17	6	2	100
5	3	20	2	50	15	6	6	100
6	4	15		47	15	4	14	100
7		10	2	34	24	14	17	100

1=unskilled worker, 2=skilled worker, 3=farmers, 4=small entrepreneurs,
3/4=farmers + small entrepreneurs, 5=lower manual workers (employees),
6=medium level employees, 7=higher occupations, 0=persons who had never worked

Because of the observed correlations between a young person's social background and education and between that person's education and occupation, a relationship between one's social background and occupation, or, more specifically, between the occupational level of the father and that of his children can be expected. Table 5.13 confirms this.

If we look more closely at the occupational levels attained by children from different social backgrounds, the most prominent trends, ranging from unskilled manual workers to the class of higher occupations, appear to be: - a decreasing percentage of persons with skilled or unskilled manual work; and an increasing percentage of persons with non-manual work on a higher level, with higher occupations or with no job until the age of 25.

Figure 5.1: Path diagram between the variables social background (sb), educational level (el) and occupational level (ol)[7]

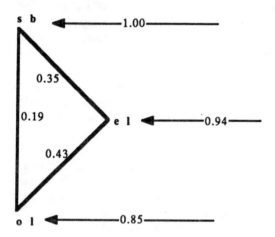

This relationship between the occupational level of young people and that of their fathers can only partially be explained by the educational levels each has attained. There must also be a strong effect of social background on the type of jobs that young people choose. This is indicated when one considers that

- the children of manual workers do more manual work and less non-manual work than could be expected from them on the basis of their education;
- the children of non-manual workers do less manual work and more non-manual work than could be expected of them when taking their levels of education into account;
- the children of medium level employees and those from higher occupational groups have held no job until the age of 25 (that is: are still studying at that age) to a greater extent than could be expected judging from, for instance, their relatively greater participation in pre-university education.

The described relations between the variables social background (sb), educational level of youth (el) and occupational level reached (ol) can be analysed with the help of summarising measures. The path diagram in Figure 5.1 reflects the main results of this analysis, which are presented below:

- there are definite transition careers to take a person from the sphere of education to that of occupation: in the Netherlands, as in most Western countries, only higher levels of education give an individual access to the higher occupations - the destiny of those who have studied at lower educational levels is work at a lower level;
- there is also a definite transition from social background to occupation - one can speak of a reproduction of social background since the occupational levels of the 1965-cohort can figure as indicators of the social background of the 1965-cohort children;
- the transition or reproduction of social background is partly affected by education which functions as a mediating mechanism; as an explanation, this indirect effect (0.15) may ultimately be reduced to differences in socialisation, and viewed to be a consequence of differences in school aptitude and in the educational aspirations among children of different social classes;
- a part of the transition or reproduction of social background cannot be explained by education (direct effect: 0.19); this part of the transition would appear to indicate that there are more direct differences between the social classes when it comes to occupational aspirations and occupational opportunities.

Conclusion

The analysis of the interrelationships between the system of education and the transition from school to work indisputably shows that education has a similar role in all the four countries. In all of them, the allocation of individuals to different positions in the system of production consequently leads to an allocation of different social positions for them (social status, social prestige and, partly, income as well). At the same time, however, historical and cultural traditions, the particular requirements of the national economies and the qualification needs of the respective economies arising from these factors form typical characteristics of each educational system.

Educational systems are not conservative unchangeable structures. They flexibly reflect changes in economic and social conditions. That is why educational systems cannot be analysed without taking these conditions into account. In all the countries mentioned in this chapter the educational systems have passed through fundamental changes during the last decade, and the aims of the reforms achieved were practically the same:

- to make the relationship between educational and labour systems closer and more consistent, thus creating better conditions for adequate youth employment;
- to make the preparation of the younger generations correspond to changing social requirements;
- to try, according to the social possibilities available, to secure favourable conditions for young people developing personal skills;
- to contribute to increasing personal opportunity for social mobility.

The link between social requirements and the abilities of the educational system to satisfy them, naturally leads to the permanent outdistance of the requirements. At the same time, substantial differences among the educational systems of the various countries could be found. For example, in their structure - in the different subdivisions covering different age cohorts of the given population; and in the different notions about the educational stages in each country. It can be seen that the first serious educational choice has to be made in the Netherlands at the age of 12, in Hungary - at the age 14, in Bulgaria at the age of 15, and in the German Democratic Republic at the age of 16. Moreover, the secondary educational level offers different possibilities for continuing with general education or vocational training. In the Netherlands, there are four different educational options: three types of general education school and one vocational school, but all of them in a strict hierarchical order; in Hungary there are three possibilities: one general, one vocational and one mixture of both; in Bulgaria, there is one general educational school and three types of professional educational schools; in the German Democratic Republic, after primary education, there are seven different school types: three vocational

121

and four general educational. Only in the latter country, does basic vocational education have a high social status.

The differences among the educational systems of the countries are a factor of primary importance for the differences in their job allocation functions. In spite of these differences, the analysis of the main interrelations of the educational and transition processes also reveals a common feature: that the level of a youth's education largely influences his occupational status. However, it is difficult to speak about social status without taking the phenomena of social mobility and social inequality into consideration. One of the ways through which these problems can be studied is, as was done here, to look at the role played by their social background. The occupational status of the father can be used as an indicator for this. It appears that a youth's social background has a strong indirect impact on his occupational status. Despite the differences in the social systems, in all countries the parental family still plays an important role in youth's transition from school to work. It has been shown that social background is important for explaining the type and level of school which young people attend. Since the school, as has been stressed before, determines the occupational status of youth, social background, in the end, indirectly influences young people's place in the occupational system. Different countries have, however, different possibilities to correct initial educational choices after leaving the school system. This also results in varied chances, at a later stage, to modify the steering force of the social background in which young people have grown up. However, here too people from different social backgrounds seem to have different opportunities.

Attention has not been paid to the mechanisms through which the parental family directly has an impact on youth's occupational choice and status. This issue will be taken up in another chapter. If a general conclusion with regard to the role of education for the transition from school to work must be drawn, it can only be said that the fundamental problem of simultaneously fulfilling education's two - basically conflicting - social requirements has not been solved: to contribute to social equality and to be efficient in terms of producing the qualifications society needs. Even recent reforms of educational systems still show all the signs of this conflict.

Notes

1. H. Fend, *Theorie der Schule* (Munich-Vienna-Baltimore, 1981), P.T. pp. 13-54.

2. See J. Venedikov, 'Problems of the self-realization of those completing secondary education' (Institute of Youth Studies, Sofia), pp. 19-22 (a report from a study kept at the information bank of the Institute of Youth Studies, Sofia) (in Bulgarian).

3. See M. Stefanov, *The student: life plans and self-realization* (Sofia, 1983), pp. 20/21 (in Bulgarian).

4. G. Neuner, *Pädagogik*, No. 9 (1985), p. 658.

5. F. Gazsó, L. Laki and P. Molnár, *Pályakezdők az iparban* (Professional Start in Industry), MSZMP KB Társadalomtudományi Intézete, Budapest, 1984.

6. From a representative sample (N = 1538), data were collected which included the father's occupation, the individual's school achievement, his vocational interests and the sequence of decision-making throughout school and in the period of transition from school to work. The aim of collecting these data was to assess the role played by the learning aptitude, interests and social background of individuals when they made career-related decisions. The data were gathered using a school test in 1965 and interviews carried out in 1970, 1974 and 1978.

7. The path diagram is based on a regression analysis of the linear (product moment) correlation coefficient among the variables social background (sb), educational level (el) and occupational level (ol).

Correlation coefficients	sb	el	ol
sb	1		
el	0.345	1	
ol	0.333	0.490	1

6

The Transition from School to Work and the Employment System. A Comparison of Experiences in Czechoslovakia, Finland, Sweden and Yugoslavia

Sonja Drobnic, Jürgen Hartmann,
Veljko Rus and Matti Vesa Volanen

Introduction

In every industrial society there must be a mechanism to regulate the demand for and supply of labour; and the transition from school to work, from job to job, and into and out of the labour force. There are at least two main ways of regulating these activities. The first one is the pattern of 'a market place', which is the same as saying the labour market process is an extension of the market of commodities. The fundamental question in the market place is that of sales and pricing. When the production process was based on mechanical machinery, it was possible to view the 'labour force' as a quasi commodity. Nowadays, however, the question is more complicated because the labour force is no longer using just its physical strength but has incorporated greatly divergent skills which are partially based on schooling into the production process. Within the educational system there are two conflicting tendencies. On the one hand, the planning of vocational education must follow the indicators of the labour market, the demand for and the supply of the labour force, while, on the other hand, the changes in the production processes must be evaluated to understand the qualificational needs of work processes.

This traditional quasi market-based way of organising the school/labour network presumes that everybody takes care of himself: each person has the responsibility to find a vocation and a job, and it very clearly depends on the individual's capacity and capability to find a place in the work force. Each person has an opportunity to select the school of his choice, profession and work organisation but, at the same time, each person also carries the entire risk. The basic structure of the transition is individualised: It is a task for the individual - not for the community - to solve the problem of finding employment. If problems exist, they do not involve this basic structure but, rather, the way in which the authorities can help an individual find a job. The labour market process, however, is not 'transparent' for an individual. The task of finding employment is a task of survival in an environment where there are very few means to manage one's life. Thus, one has rights in a situation where the means necessary for their realisation are not available. What you own is your labour force - qualified or not. On the one hand, you can as an owner do what you want with this property. On the other hand you have to sell this labour force to make your living.

The other way to manage the transition processes which take place between schools, jobs, as well as in and out of the labour force is based on the idea of social guarantee. The labour market process is seen as a non-transparent process which is impossible for an individual to handle or to understand. The network between schooling and production is the central relation. The political objective is to minimise the effect of the market process: there will be no 'unplanned' transitions. When you choose your school and line of vocational education, you, at the same time, choose your first job in a factory or a firm. There is no labour market process as an 'invisible hand' driving the labour force to be flexible in accordance with the needs of production. This means that schooling itself has to help form this kind of flexibility. There is quite a strong cross-pressure within the educational process itself: this pressure has to reflect the actual needs of production and it must also be a process which forms general abilities in individuals to encounter the changing tasks of working life.

Under the system of social guarantee, the responsibility for transitions can be installed and regulated between individuals and social institutions according to the economic situation. An individual is a citizen not only as the owner of his/her labour, but his/her possibilities for managing the transitions are correlated to the social institutions. While one may not have all the possibilities of choice, one does have the privilege of being protected by social institutions. The task of 'finding one's place in working life' is a task which is divided between the citizen and the social institutions. The social institutions are usually conservative and they do not see new possibilities as 'realistic', rather, they see them as impossible under 'objective' situations. This results in pressure between what is possible and what is impossible. The system of social guarantee creates social security for an individual but also easily develops social limitations.

The school/labour network operates between social institutions. Government regulation of the transitions between institutions can be done via three different processes: 1) economic planning, 2) the terms of the labour market, and 3) monetary policy. If we look at the structure of transitions at the same time - the school/labour network - and the main tools of regulation, we get the following hypothetical models of transition (see Figure 6.1):

Figure 6.1: Models of transition

Tools of regulation	The structure of the school-labour network	
	social guarantee	individual risk
economic planning	1	2
labour market	4	3

The figure suggests hypothetic models for the transition from school to work:

1. The demand for labour is mainly regulated by the planning of production, and the transitions are based on social guarantee. This model is typical for socialist countries.
2. The demand for labour is mainly regulated by the planning of the production process, but the transitions are mostly based on individual risk. This situation is most clearly seen in Yugoslavia.
3. The regulation of the demand for labour is mainly based on operations in the labour market, and the transitions are taken care of by individuals. This is a standard situation in West European capitalist countries.
4. The regulation of the demand for labour is mainly based on operations in the labour market, but the transitions are guaranteed by social institutions. The Nordic countries are

somewhere between model three and model four.

In the following pages, the problems of the transition from school to work in Czechoslovakia, Yugoslavia, Finland and Sweden are looked at. In these countries, the tools of regulation and the structure of the school/labour network are based on different solutions. After basic information is given on each country, the qualitative differences of the transition from school to work in each one is evaluated.

Model One: Czechoslovakia

Planned regulation of employment

Czechoslovakia and some of the other socialist countries provide an example for illustrating the process of the transition of young people from school to work under conditions marked by full employment and a permanent shortage of manpower in many sectors and professions of the national economy.

This situation gives rise to a specific type of transition process - from work to work and from school to work. Once we describe the need 'to find some sort of solution' as a problem of the first order and the need 'to find a satisfactory solution' as a problem of the second order, then it becomes clear that due to the prevailing demand for manpower, problems of the first order are shifting primarily towards the employer system which needs to meet its own manpower demands and hence is bound to play an active role in manpower recruitment policies. Problems of the first order only confront applicants seeking employment in attractive professions, i.e. in occupational spheres attracting a large contingent of applicants. At the same time, the situation reflects the mounting role of the state which, acting as the representative of social ownership, controls the use of all resources, including manpower.

The trend affecting the social demand for work in the Czechoslovak economy of the post-war period was governed by two decisive factors: the relatively advanced basis of the domestic economy and the extremely fast process of nationalisation of practically all production capacities in industry and in agriculture on the basis of state or co-operative ownership. As a result, a unified system of a centrally controlled economy, using short-term and long-term plans, came into existence. However, as economic mechanisms failed to exert the required pressure conducive to rational resource management, a challenging situation arose in the sphere of resources, where most enterprises found it easier to tackle the ever rigorous tasks by expanding standing capacities. The expansive line of development followed in creating industry absorbed manpower resources released from the agricultural sphere and gradually engulfed all inner reserves.

The permanent shortage of manpower necessitated the adoption of a more consistent strategy of state control over processes connected with the distribution of manpower. The manpower quota for individual employer organisations are therefore specified by the plan and the scale of priorities is also applied in the different delimitation of the territories for the recruitment of new manpower for different enterprises and different sectors of the national economy. More advantageous wage conditions and other material incentives are typical strategies practised by the state to boost interest in employment spheres which make up the less attractive professions. To ensure the desirable amount of migration, the state employs indirect stimuli such as a more efficient public transportation system, better services, the construction of preschool facilities for children, and the like. Recruitment and retention[1] of the labour force, the rational distribution of manpower within the organisation, qualification improvement and professional growth are all activities which constitute the basis of the plans of personnel management and social development that are elaborated on and detailed in all work organisations.

From extensive to intensive development

However, the seemingly idyllic situation in the employment sphere reveals, on closer scrutiny, one formidable problem. The current situation is the outcome of the extensive character of economic development based on an upward trend in resource consumption. Intensifying the rate of economic dynamism - a task confronting all socialist countries in the 1980s - presupposes a consistent implementation of the intensification strategy which seeks to achieve a more efficient utilisation of resources, to encourage scientific and technological progress and to promote technical and technological innovations.

Considering the factual exhaustion of manpower reserves, the young generation crossing the line to a productive economic age represents society's one and only potential source of supply and reproduction of work capacity. The distribution of manpower resources is systematically monitored and controlled on a planned basis. This is a sphere where society pursues two concurrent objectives: to ensure - in compliance with the expanding range of possibilities - better standards of education in individual generations as a means of personality development[2] and to control and direct the professional training of the young generation in a way which best meets the needs of the national economy.

Regulating educational choice

Regulation of employment thus starts with the control of the structure and content of secondary school education. The school system assumes responsibility for the education and training of young people for future professions. This strategy is practised early and already starts at the level of the eight-year elementary school. Goals and objectives specified for this level include the aim that education should be geared towards the promotion of young people's positive attitude to labour. Completion of elementary education is connected with the first phase of educational and vocational choice. In the past, only a certain section of elementary school leavers directly entered the work process (see Table 6.1).

Table 6.1: The distribution of young people after completion of compulsory school attendance

	1976	1980	1984
General secondary schools	37.4	39.7	36.6
Secondary vocational schools	56.2	56.3	60.6
Workplaces	4.1	2.8	1.0
Continuation of basic education	1.2	0.5	1.7
Incapable of assignment	1.0	0.6	
Non-assigned	0.1	0.1	0.1
Total (in thousands)	218 249	245 166	224 590

At present, each pupil chooses one of the types of secondary school open to him/her. Grammar schools and secondary vocational schools offer complete secondary school education oriented towards further study at the university level and ultimately towards the exercise of a profession involving intellectual work. Secondary vocational apprentice-training centres offer training leading to skilled manual occupations.

An instrument of state control in the assignment of young people to future professions is the regulation of the capacities specific to individual types of schools, study programmes and vocational training programmes mediated through planned quotas of newly enrolled students and apprentices. Roughly 40% of all youngsters in a population year enroll for study at grammar schools and secondary vocational schools. Interest in more demanding forms of education is, of course, substantially higher. While the growing educational standard and the modernisation of the content of instruction give young people access to new, attractive professions in the developing production branches, society is confronted with the need to provide viable conditions for manpower reproduction in less attractive, yet socially useful, spheres of employment. The mismatch between the professional aspirations of the young generation and the needs of society thus manifests itself early - in the initial phase of choosing a specific educational path - and is not postponed until the final confrontation with the employment system.

The state makes systematic efforts to dovetail the distribution of children to different types of secondary schools in compliance with their innate abilities and talent while paying maximum attention to their specific professional interests. The promotion of better standards of professional orientation among children and parents is the central purpose of the current system of vocational guidance operating through school counsellors for vocational advice. For an objective appraisal of child's natural aptitude and abilities, parents may decide to avail themselves of the services offered by district psycho-pedagogical counselling centres.

The first phase of the educational and, to a certain extent, vocational choice is fraught with specific problems. The primary interest of society is to give a sound estimate of the future professional need and to quantify this estimate in terms of the respective numerical quotas specifying the permissible number of students in the respective fields of study and, no less important, to transform this estimate into the concrete content of instruction and vocational training. Improving the efficiency of the system of capacity-planning and improving the content of the process of training and education in compliance with the requirements of optimal professional application are the two tasks preoccupying the state institutions.

Viewed from the vantage point of young people, the crucial problem resides in an individual taking the first step in decision-making at an age marked by social immaturity and when some of the prerequisites for a responsible and, in this sense, free decision are still lacking. Parental aspirations and interests - not always consonant with the child's natural abilities - are very much in evidence at this stage of decision-making.[3] A social advantage is the open-ended nature of the entire educational system which offers all young people access to alternative educational paths thus providing them with the opportunity to complete their training and education. This also includes access to university study and mitigates the rigour of the initial constraints restricting educational chances.[4]

Of major relevance for the actual process of transition of young people from school to work is the impact of the employment system on the system of vocational training in terms of the acquisition of professional qualifications and the timing and particular mode of relation arising between the apprentice and/or student and the future employer.

The impact of the employment system on vocational training programmes implemented at secondary-school and university levels can roughly be described as follows: branch ministries formulate the requirements placed on students training for different specialisations. These requirements provide a basis for the specification of the quotas for the acceptance of students in the respective fields of specialisation. Manpower recruitment policies also involve periods of infield practice organised for the students by enterprises, production units and other work organisations; furthermore, enterprises share in the specification and delimitation of subjects to be covered by diploma theses and, in this respect, provide conditions conducive to their implementation; finally, there is the system of enterprise-sponsored grants. The student receiving such a grant accepts the commitment to work for a certain number of years in the sponsor's enterprise (the obligatory period of employment is never longer than the total duration of study). The vital bond with the future place of employment is thus forged right at the training stage, and most students develop an intimate relationship with the target vocation while still at school.

The school actively assists the process of professional integration by pooling information on potential careers and prospective openings in the employment sphere and by systematically monitoring the process of work allocation in the group of secondary school leavers and university students. Just as in other countries, in Czechoslovakia, too, the student's own interest and resourcefulness in making use of unconventional modes of information acquisition play an important role in the choice of future employment.

Somewhat different is the situation characterising young people training for skilled manual occupations. Secondary vocational apprentice training centres are established and financed directly by the branch levels of economic management and state control. The ministry of education controls the operation and activity of secondary vocational apprentice training centres by providing conceptual and methodological guidance, by appointing the staff of teachers and instructors and by supplying the required media of instruction. The permissible quotas of apprentices for individual vocational training centres and different types of apprentice training are specified on the basis of resource allocation and budgeting by the state plan. The enterprises themselves also exert a good deal of initiative in the recruitment of future manpower from within the ranks of apprentice trainees. They organise periods of infield training and on-the-job training. In applying for enrollment in courses of training offered by specific vocational training centres, the school leaver also deliberately chooses the future employer, although, according to recent legal regulations, a completed term of apprenticeship in no way implies an obligation for the apprentice to enter employment in a specific work organisation. However, the enterprise can - and indeed does make full use of this possibility in practice - conclude a contract of employment with the apprentice after completion of the second year of training (after the conclusion of the period of compulsory school attendance) according to the general principles of the Labour Code. The contract of employment specifies the day on which the apprentice enters employment, the future work-place and the type of work. As theoretical training and practical training are combined in the syllabus of vocational training centres, transition to the future work-place is a smooth natural process.

In a situation in which most professions are characterised by the predominance of manpower demand over manpower offer, most school and university graduates enter employment right after completing their studies. In the past, certain difficulties were encountered by grammar school leavers not accepted for university study. This problem was mitigated under the recent education reform with the polytechnisation of the syllabuses followed by the setting up of Czechoslovak grammar schools and by the introduction of a specialised subject of instruction called 'Fundamentals of production and vocational training'. The latter offers the possibility to acquire qualifications for specific skilled manual occupations and for functions which are to be exercised in the sphere of technical management. Problems occur in some cases, especially in the group of university graduates. These are due to an inadequate assessment of the actual need of the professionals in question. These problems are tackled by the state administration in close cooperation with branch organisations, and remedial action includes the creation of new employment opportunities and the transition to employment in related branches. Certain disproportions may also arise in connection with the territorial distribution of the leavers due to their reluctance to migrate.

In general, however, it remains the case that the confrontation between young people's professional aspirations and the needs of the employment system occurs prior to the inception of vocational training and thus proves to be an efficient mechanism of optimalisation. Apart from this, of course, the process of vocational training itself shapes, to a considerable extent, the aprofessional aspirations of young people in conformity to the requirements of the prospective vocation. The effects of this adaptation process should not be overrated; if the gap between desire and reality is considerable, the desirable effect is not achieved. Quantitatively, this problem can be described as a problem of a lower order - a problem affecting only a minor section of young people.

In the context of conditions in which the transition from school to first employment is not a social problem, society's interest as well as the individual's interest concentrate on the subsequent phases of professional integration, on the process of work adaptation, and on the development and application of the qualifications acquired. The congruence or incongruence between acquired and required education, between the qualifications acquired by training and the profession actually exercised, figure prominently among the topics under study in employment statistics. The latest data indicate that the current situation still leaves a good deal to be desired and cannot be described as optimal.

One of the factors influencing the present state of affairs is the professional and employer mobility in the first years of a professional career in which, despite the assertion of social interests, personal interests and individual preferences of all shades and nuances play a considerable part. According to the data obtained during research into the life careers of young people in an 18- to 29-years-old age group, almost one fifth changed their original profession; the mobility curve reached the culmination point roughly after three years of work. More frequent is the change of work organisation determined for 25% of young workers and in a number of cases repeatedly. The optimalisation trend in the initial years of employment attests to a multi-directional process. Nevertheless, it is a process in which transitions from physical work to intellectual work, from the production sphere to non-production activities, from semi-skilled work to skilled work clearly predominate.

Table 6.2: Social structure of the age groups of young Czechs in 1970 and 1980 (%)

Age group	Year	Economically active	Students secondary schools	Apprentices	House- wives	Invalids, others
15-19	1970	38.3	30.7	27.7	1.1	2.2
	1980	29.4	36.4	32.2	0.7	1.3
20-24	1970	85.1	6.2	0.1	7.1	1.5
	1980	85.0	10.5	0.1	3.0	1.4
25-29	1970	88.7	0.3	0.0	9.8	1.2
	1980	94.5	0.5	0.0	3.8	1.2

Model Two: Yugoslavia

Introduction

Yugoslavia is a country with a mixed economic system where market and plan mechanisms coexist; this also influences the transition from school to work. The importance of both mechanisms has varied over the years. In the 1980s, new self-management regulations which coordinate the school system, the employment system and the transition between them were introduced.

The efficiency of regulation can be considered from different points of view, but if we take youth unemployment in Yugoslavia into account, especially the proportion of people who are seeking a job for the first time, it seems that the existing mechanisms have not been able to adequately cope with transition problems (see Table 6.3).

Table 6.3: The proportion of young job seekers and unemployed persons in Yugoslavia seeking their first job compared to the total number of unemployed (%)

Year	unemployed under 25 years	unemployed, seeking a job for the first time
1957	37.4	26.3
1960	43.3	33.3
1965	41.9	33.1
1970	46.9	51.2
1975	54.4	59.8
1980	55.6	68.2
1982	57.5	68.7

The present trend is especially problematic because of the relatively high educational level of unemployed persons. In 1957, only 18.4% of all unemployed were qualified workers or workers with secondary or university education. In 1970, this number increased to 28.1% and, at the beginning of the 1980s, over 50% of the unemployed belonged to these categories. The work demand has not followed the increasing qualification level of young job seekers; as a result, the qualification level of the unemployed is now higher than the qualification level of employed workers.

These unfavourable figures are not the result of one fixed, unchangeable regulative system. On the contrary, several different regulative mechanisms have been used in Yugoslavia.

The Development of Employment Regulation

Plan regulation

Immediately after the World War II, a state decree administratively allocated jobs to school leavers. The labour force was regulated by the state plan during the first post-war decade, even in the initial period after the introduction of the self-management system in 1950. During a short period of five years (1950-1955), Yugoslavia created an unusual system where self-management and state regulation of the labour force co-existed.

After 1955, the labour market mechanism was fully established. Individuals became owners of their own labour and had unlimited freedom of choice in schooling and employment. This exclusively individual (or private) ownership over labour coincided with a predominantly public ownership of the means of production (Tanko, 1985). The conflicts between these two structural parameters represent the basic framework for Yugoslav manpower regulation.

Anarchic regulation of the labour market

Public ownership of the means of production presupposes that all members of society have equal rights to use these means of production. In reality, however, these means are almost exclusively managed at the collective level and individuals can maximise their own benefits only through their participation in work organisations. In this way work organisations become the main regulators of the labour force and the main subject on the labour market as well. They try to maximise their own particular interests (profits, high wages, market power, high job security) not only by the appropriation of goods on the basis of their own work contribution, but also by monopolistic prices, technical rents, natural rents, and so on. This system of 'collective profit sharing' creates great disproportions in the labour market and contributes to the anarchic regulation of the latter. The consequences of this are numerous: great wage differences between branches for the same quality and quantity of jobs (Korosic, 1985), a regionally segmented labour market with uneven regional rates of employment and unemployment, a segmentated labour market on the level of work organisations (Svetlik, 1984) and increasing intergenerational employment discriminations (Drobnic, 1984a).

The segmentation of the labour market caused by the particularistic interests of work organisations is especially damaging in the field of employment. The particularistic employment policy of work organisation tends to maximise job security for their own workers through capital intensive investments, restrictive hiring and high solidarity among employees, domination of internal promotion and non-dismissal of workers who are already employed.

In periods of recession, this employment policy practically closes the door to school leavers creating, at the same time, high levels of underemployment inside work organisations. Newcomers on the labour market become highly discriminated against. One could argue that the public ownership of the means of production has been transformed into a group ownership.

The resocialisation of the labour market

Because of the above-mentioned disfunctions, a resocialisation of the labour market became unavoidable. An additional reason for changes was the recession in West European countries. In the late 1960s, Yugoslavia experienced labour emigration on a mass scale. But when the immigration countries tightened their immigration control to protect their own labour markets, this labour emigration was stopped and the problems of a surplus labour force became more critical. From 1973 on, the rate of unemployment has increased remarkably, particularly among educated youth, and within the less developed regions of Yugoslavia.

The resocialisation of the labour market started with two significant changes: the introduction of Self-Management Associations of Interests (SAI) and the reform of secondary education.

Self-management associations of interest

The first change was a structural one. The idea behind the introduction of SAIs was to diminish the role of the state and the market in the production and allocation of certain social services and goods. Workers and citizens should, on the basis of self-management, agree on financing the health service, education, science, cultural life and the social security system. SAIs are combined bodies of two assemblies: one assembly is composed of delegates who represent the interests of those work organisations producing certain services, the other assembly consists of delegates who represent those organisations which are the main potential users of services. Assemblies of the SAI for education and employment should create yearly contracts for the programme of educational activity and yearly budgets for its implementation. The SAI should therefore become an institute for the direct contractual regulation of the labour force; it should replace, at the some time, the state plan and the market as regulators. Figure 6.2 presents the regulation of the labour force after the establishment of the SAI and according to the theory and formal rules which apply.

Figure 6.2: Self-Management Association of Interest

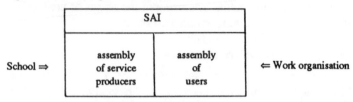

During the last ten years, this system has demonstrated a number of weaknesses. Obviously, direct contractual regulation between school and the work system cannot completely replace market and state plan regulators. Work organisations are still interested in maximising their own profit, therefore they try to externalise the costs for education and other social services as much as possible. The result of this is subfinanced social services, especially schools. On the other hand, schools do not like to restrict their programmes and capacities to the actual needs of work organisations since they are aware that their function is not only to provide work organisations with labour but also to reproduce the national educational system. Work organisations, however, are not willing to finance this.

These tensions between the pragmatic needs of industrial work organisations and the broader cultural needs of society are also reflected in the scholarship system in Yugoslavia. The proportion of scholarships for particular occupations that are granted directly by work organisations is increasing. On the other hand, the number of 'social scholarships', which are dependent only on the social standing of the family, is decreasing. The aim of this trend is clearly to orientate pupils and students towards occupations in which the supply of workers is insufficient. Consequently, there are usually many scholarships for schooling of short duration and not enough for people who want to go to secondary schools that last 4-5 years or to university.

The reform of secondary education

The school reform introduced in the late 1970s is another change which is supposed to socialise the labour market. With the reform of secondary education, preparatory secondary schools such as gymnasiums were abolished. The main goal of the school reform was to have all secondary schools prepare pupils for certain vocations.

At the same time, the apprenticeship system (the so-called 'double system') was also abolished. For all secondary schools, a new standardised programme of general education was established for the first year of secondary schooling. After the first year, programmes are oriented towards preparation for certain skills. It was foreseen that around 80% of secondary school leavers would be employed after leaving secondary school and that only 20% of them would directly continue their education at colleges or universities.

The reform of secondary schools was supposed to create a more standardised general education in order to decrease cultural differences between previous gymnasiums and vocational schools. Besides providing for greater equalisation, the school reform was to become more responsive to the needs of work organisations by preparing vocational profiles which could be immediately useful to them. In accordance with these intentions, 70% of all scholarships should be granted for technical studies and natural sciences and only 30% should be available for students in the humanities and social sciences.

This school reform caused a general revolt among parents, school teachers and intellectuals all over the country. It was argued that the reform was anachronistic in trying to carry out a kind of reindustrialisation of education at a time when industrialisation as a way of modernisation had already demonstrated negative rather than positive effects. The consequences of the school reform have been, in fact, predominantly negative:

- School reform has not brought about cultural destratification but has rather transferred this from society into each particular school.
- Due to the orientation of schools towards vocational training, school programmes have become extremely diversified. This reorientation substantially increased the costs of schooling just at a time when Yugoslavia experienced a severe economic crisis. The lack of money is reflected in insufficient school equipment and low wages for the teachers.
- The school reform was introduced under the assumption that the old dual system of secondary education was the main

cause for the increasing structural unemployment among youth. However, a recent study of unemployment in Slovenia shows that the unemployment, caused by the occupational discrepancies between vacancies and unemployed, represents only one fourth of total unemployment.

- The elasticity of the supply of labour has decreased.
- The reform of secondary education has been followed by a reform of higher education and at the university level. This new reform threatens to lower the intellectual level of university programmes and to reduce the autonomy of the university itself.

It is now estimated that the school reform itself has contributed to the rapid growth of youth unemployment in the 1980s, although it is not reasonable to accuse the school reform of being the single cause for this.

As a reaction to these disfunctions, new mechanisms of regulation were introduced. Their main characteristic is an increasing interventionism of the state into the school and the employment system. Such interventions are mainly restrictive, such as: obligatory retirement of older workers; obligation of work organisations to employ school leavers in proportion to the number of already employed workers, regardless of economic needs; restrictions on overtime work; administrative changes in the definition of unemployment, and so on.

In addition to state interventionism, opposing theories are also growing. One group of theorists argues for the abolition of individual ownership of labour, or, at the least, to substantially restrict the freedom of choice for schooling and jobs. Such restrictions would allow the 'anarchic' behaviour of the labour force to be diminished and common goals of employment policy could be better achieved (Suvar, 1977).

A second group attacks this suggestion, arguing that it is incompatible with the liberal nature of Yugoslav socialism and suggests instead the deindustrialisation of the education process. This current of opinion argues for the introduction of general secondary education and the transfer of vocational training to the work organisations (Rus, 1985b).

The Future Prospects

Apart from the disfunctions of the school reform, the problems of the overall regulation of the labour force in Yugoslavia are also unresolved. Temporary state interventionism, which tries to compensate for the disfunctions of SAIs and school reform, is certainly not a satisfying solution. In the long run, only those solutions seem to be acceptable which establish the transfer from school to work in such a way that the mechanisms of transition would function as a system of conflict resolution between partly, or even completely, opposing professional, personal and job demands.

The most acceptable transfer from school to work will probably be established through a self-employment system - i.e. through the self-initiative of individuals. However, self-initiative will not be sufficient since the employment process is becoming too complex. Assistance from other social agencies is also necessary for the successful transfer from school to work. State agencies should assure, therefore, minimal programmes and take care of marginal or handicapped groups, while the SAIs should be reorganised in such a way that they would receive external support from the unions, chambers of commerce and professional associations. These agencies have fairly extensive bargaining power and could revitalise the whole employment system. Their participation in bargaining might contribute to more qualitatively satisfying agreements between the assembly of producers and the assembly of users within the SAIs.

In short, the discussion about feasible and acceptable mechanisms of transfer from school to work still continues. At present, it is argued that a more comprehensive and integrated system of guided self-employment should be developed by taking into account and combining the self-initiative of individuals, state agencies and regulation through SAIs.

Models Three and Four: The Examples of Sweden and Finland

Youth on the Swedish Labour Market

For a period of more than thirty years after World War II, the Swedish labour market was characterised by a labour shortage which had to be compensated for by immigration labour. During the same period, both unions and employers agreed on a labour-market policy which not only accepted lay-offs at non-profitable work-places but also facilitated structural changes directed towards higher national productivity and thereby a higher standard of living for all Swedes. For young people, the problem was to obtain qualified training to enable the individual to adapt to the ongoing process of change.

In the 1960s and 1970s, there was a firm belief in Sweden that all unemployment problems could be solved by either retraining or obtaining additional educational qualifications. Unemployment was caused, according to this belief, only by the mismatch between the individual characteristics of job-seekers and the needs of production, not by structural constraints. To cure unemployment, especially among youth, one only needed to expand the training system. But despite a rise in the quantity and quality of youth education during the 1970s, which lowered the general number of young people on the labour market, youth unemployment continued to grow.

The exclusion of 16 and 17 year-olds from the labour market was openly declared when the Swedish parliament transferred the responsibility for this age group from the Labour Market Administration (AMS) to the local school authorities without raising the official age at which youth could leave school. (Magnussen, 1981). The reason for this dramatic step can be found in a number of factors lowering the chances for this age group to obtain gainful employment on the open labour market. The adoption of an Employment Security Act in 1974 - which improved the security of employment for those already employed - together with industrial safety regulations that prohibited the employment of youth under 18 in many jobs and for certain hours of the day, the rise in women's employment, and an adjustment of young people's wages to almost the same level as that of experienced workers, were all factors which contributed to a decline in the number of employed youth during the 1970s.

The transfer of the responsibility for unemployed youth from the labour-market authorities to the school system opened a new era in Swedish labour-market policy. At the same time, the labour-market administration was a strictly centralised organisation and constituted an instrument with which the government could directly influence regional and local markets, and even affect policy-making on the local level.

The rising costs of relief programmes and the traditional method of creating employment locally, forced the government to look for other solutions. This became even more urgent as a number of young had discovered that it was quite profitable to leave school at 16 and immediately receive a guaranteed income, which in 1975 was about 2,500 kronor ($600) per month from a relief programme, whereas the grant for continued study was 250 kronor ($60) per month in the same year (Hartmann, 1977). In 1985, there were at least five different programmes which were keeping young people aged 16 to 18 out of the unemployment category. The programmes point out the great variety of intervention measures used, and the levels of remuneration paid to individual participants and to the organisations which employ youth. The reason for these differences becomes clear if we bear in mind that the majority of young people covered by the programmes are those who do not wish to continue secondary education. Even though the Swedish government, in its 1980 Youth Bill, had envisaged a 100% participation of all 16 year-olds in regular secondary education (Magnussen, 1981), in 1984, about 9% of all youth under 18 took part in some kind of external youth follow-up programme administered by municipal school authorities.

As many youngsters are quite reluctant to stay in any type of continued schooling, a number of municipalities have created special youth centres, often run in co-operation with other organisations or public agencies. Here, with the help of counsellors, vocational training assistants, welfare officers and psychologists, individualised plans are developed to overcome young people's resistance to further training, or to find possibilities for them to enter the labour market.

In 1984, the unemployment rate of those aged 20 to 24 was more than three times the rate for those aged 25 to 64, but from age 20 onwards, no special programmes are offered for unemployed youth. Instead, the usual instruments of labour market policy are applied. That means that relief work or retraining measures are connected with a remuneration enabling the participants to live on a quite normal Swedish income (5,000-8,000 kronor per month), depending on their previous occupation and income. According to labour-market statistics, about 2% of the 20- to 25-years-old age group were engaged in relief work in February 1985 and 2.5% in labour-market training, whereas about 5% were openly unemployed (AMS statistics, 1985). In an international context, these unemployment figures are rather low, and extensive follow-up by the labour market authorities prevents a long duration of open unemployment. However, as has been pointed out by several researchers, there is a tendency for young unemployed people to shift between different types of programmes without being able to get a job on the free labour market. They are caught in what has been called an 'unemployment career'.

While Swedish labour-market policy seems to be very effective in taking care of unemployed individuals and the variety of programmes and benefits guarantee a decent income, the creation of new employment has to be accomplished elsewhere. Measures such as guaranteed employment in a youth team are often short-term solutions governed more by financial considerations than by real concern about the needs and aspirations of young people. Furthermore, most of the measures are based on a traditional economic model that promotes material production for the market and neglects the need for services and for a functioning network of social relations at the local community level. Instead of integrating youth into the general labour market, employment programmes tend to create their own career patterns, thereby trapping young people in a system of policies and regulations which they find difficult to understand and use for their individual requirements.

The Employment Situation of Finnish Youth

The Finnish transition to an industrialised society, which is actually still in process, has been one of the quickest in Europe. The industrial society is only finding its forms, preindustrial structures (ways of living and thinking, social institutions) are dissolving, and the breakout of so-called 'new technology' has brought forth new challenges associated with the 'information' or 'postindustrial' society. In other words, Finland has a rather heterogeneous employment structure.

The age structure of Finland's population also varies a great deal. The large age groups born after the war have already entered working life. These age groups caused many bottlenecks as they were going through the educational system. In the 1970s the number of 16 year-olds is declining, but it will increase again during the 1980s. The population peak of the post-war baby boom will change from young adults to the middle-aged in the 1980s.

In two decades, the economically active members of Finland's population have increased significantly. At the same time, the number of students attending school has also gone up to 12% of the population. In 1980, the change has been most radical among the 15 to 19 year-olds: three out of four were studying at the beginning of the 1980s.

In the 1970s, labour force participation was quite stable in Finland, ranging between 63% and 67%, with unemployment between 4% and 7%. Unemployment among the 15 to 19 year-olds has been over 15% since 1975; the older age group (20-24) has been in a somewhat better position: unemployment has wavered between 7% and 10%. The duration of unemployment has increased during the last ten years; the proportion of short unemployment has clearly decreased but longer periods of unemployment have increased. Almost every vocationally educated young adult found his/her first job within 2-6 months; of these women have had a little more success. At the same time, about half of the vocationally educated young people experienced some unemployment during the first five years after school and about two out of ten had spent an entire year looking for a job (Volanen, 1984a).

Finding a job in Finland is the responsibility of each individual, and this is also true for young school leavers. They are confronted with the usual problems of a 'free' labour market situation: first they form their own vocational identity at school (including expectations and qualifications), then they have to look for a job on the labour market that would match their vocational identity and, finally, they have to try to get such a job. Of course, at every stage, there are social institutions to guide them, but the young also have to find their own way through these institutions.

Research done by one of the authors (Volanen, 1984a) has shown that about half of the young people are more or less successful in finding a job corresponding to their training and education within a reasonable period of time. Three out of ten, however, had to take any job they could get and, therefore, frequently changed their jobs, which led to a feeling of being unsuccessful. One out of ten, either through a change in education or through a change in job, managed to find a satisfying place in the employment system. The problem of vocational identity is crystalised in the process of transition from school to work. On the one hand, the labour market process demands the individual solve the problem of unemployment but, on the other hand, the labour market process is very difficult to handle by individual action.

In response to the youth employment problems experienced from the 1970s onwards, the entire Finnish educational system is undergoing reforms. A comprehensive school has been introduced, the development of the curriculum is in progress and one of its themes is to increase the connections between school and working life. In secondary-level general education, a course-based study method has just been introduced in the upper levels of secondary school. A reform of vocational education is at the stage of implementation; its basic aim is to form broadly-based educational lines to cover several occupations in working life. This means that an attempt is being made to increase vocational flexibility (mobility and substitution) by combining training for several related vocations. In this way, education is then related to more and different jobs. This somewhat technical solution to the problem of vocational flexibility is more a reaction to the serious troubles in labour market processes than to the development of productional processes, although the latter seem to imply a need for greater flexibility as well (Grootings *et al.*, 1988).

In recent years, the member of guidance counsellors at schools and employment bureaux has also increased, and there are a great number of different administrative programmes for helping young people get additional schooling or a job for at least a six- or twelve-month period. The flattest step in Finland has been that the main responsibility for the 16 and 17 year-olds has been transferred from the labour market authorities to the school administration. At the same time, there is an attempt to form close information networks between the vocational institutions and work organisations.

One very important reaction of the Finnish government has been to increase the social guarantee for young people. The latest step in this area is a proposal for a Law of Employment. The aim of this guarantee is to arrange for a job or further education for everyone under 20 and to interrupt long-term unemployment (over 12 months). This proposal was under discussion in the Finnish parliament in the autumn of 1987. It means that communes or the state have to find a job or a place of education for everybody.

The situation in Finland is rather problematic. To reduce unemployment, the country has used several administrative tools via labour market processes for many years. Nevertheless, unemployment has been increasing. In 1987, the rate of unemployment was, on the average, between 6.9% and 7.5% the rate has been higher among the younger generations, between 9% and 15%.

Almost all the tools used by the government to reduce unemployment are related to labour market processes. A solution to unemployment on this basis means hard pressures on the young unemployed to take any kind of job whether or not it is related to their vocational orientation or education. At the same time, the differentiation in the production process becomes increasingly based on the results of education. This means that there must be some kind of attachment to some aspect of the vocational area in which young people are interested. If the aim to reduce unemployment is seen only as a labour market problem, it easily turns into a superficial problem: to work or not to work. The problem of transition from school to work is, also in Finland, not merely the problem of how to find a job for every school leaver. The basic problems are, what kind of a job and how to co-ordinate young people and the employment system. Within this perspective, at least four difficult questions of a broader political nature need to be answered.

-   First, will it be possible for Finland to make the transition from an industrial society to an information society without radically changing the relationship among education, the labour market and production? The fast transition towards an industrial society has not yet come to an end in Finland and the pre-industrial way of life and thinking still exists. At the same time, the information society has arrived. The transition from pre-industrial to industrial society has been paid for with high occupational, regional and social mobility. It has been extremely difficult for the education system to soften these processes.
-   Second, how will the relationship between education and the production process be resolved? The tools for regulating the labour market have proven to be ineffective when it comes to solving this basic problem. The use of a regulative guidance system easily turns against its own aim, from guiding the flow of pupils from school to school and from school to work, to controlling the process. This strategy can be successful only if there are some other social mechanisms which produce the motives for schooling and labour. Short-term solutions on the basis of 'anything is better than nothing' have a negative effect on motivational development, while technological and

147

organisational development in the employment system are asking for higher motivation and involvement.

- Third, the blueprint for our education reforms is based on the concept for an industrial society. The aim is for everyone to get a vocational education, and broad-profile vocational schooling is formed according to the industrial division of labour. However, given the changes in the production processes, it is impossible to promise young people educated in a vocation that they will have an occupation related to their schooling. The chances that they will be frustrated and disappointed will, therefore, increase. Furthermore, it will probably be impossible to use the education system to soften the pressure of international economic competition.

- Fourth, sooner or later there will have to be a choice between supporting the law of unemployment, which forces people to remain where they are, and using market forces in the spirit of 'new liberalism', which means that mobility (vocational and regional) of the labour force should increase. What will Finland choose? Economical development and its regulation is heading in the direction of using market forces in the spirit of 'new liberalism'. At the same time, the country is trying to stop unemployment with laws. There is, therefore, a latent conflict between economic policy and social policy.

Conclusion

The four national cases described here suggest that normatively different mechanisms of employment are converging at the empirical level. Although, in the West European countries, employment systems are mainly regulated through the market, they are also regulated by different interventions of public and state bodies. The opposite might also be said for East European countries: although they are predominantly regulated by state plans, they leave some manoeuvring space to the individuals: such as, freedom of choice in selecting a school, a profession and a work organisation. The combined regulation of employment by plan and by market is a convergence which can be observed in all four cases.

Such a mixed regulation of employment processes is institutionally and empirically most visible in the case of Yugoslavia, where the private ownership of the labour force offers employees the right to choose their school, profession and work organisation; but where, at the same time, this individual freedom is limited by interorganisational, contractual relationships which are derived from attempts to co-ordinate the 5-year plans of work organisations.

In Sweden and in Finland, the labour market is controlled and managed through the so-called integrated Welfare State and based on active employment policy programmes. The state not only takes care of unemployed persons by financially supporting them and facilitating their re-training but also by establishing some programmes which create an additional number of working places; in this way, the rate of unemployment is kept below 5%.

The opposite can be said for Czechoslovakia: here state employment regulation offers individual employees increasingly greater room for manoeuvre to choose a profession and work organisation. State regulation of employment does not, therefore, eliminate individual initiatives for looking for alternative jobs.

The combined regulation of employment through plans and market might be evaluated from two points of view: that of feasibility and that of acceptability. The Scandinavian combined employment system might be rated as highly feasible and also highly acceptable. This preferred combination of market and state regulation of employment is a consequence of a functional differentiation of both regulators: state and public agencies take care of distributive justice, while the market takes care of efficient or feasible allocation of manpower.

The preference for such a functional differentiation between state and market regulation can be observed in the endeavours of Sweden and Finland to transfer responsibility for employment from youth to public agencies. In Finland, the Law of Employment should assure state guarantees either for a job or re-training for all those below the age of 20, while in Sweden, the school is obliged to take care of all those below the age of 25. By such measures, marginalisation of youth is prevented while the functioning of the labour market as such is not endangered. Just the opposite: its social disfunctions are eliminated.

In Yugoslavia, these two functions are not clearly separated and, therefore, the contamination of both is unavoidable. Overprotected employees and underprotected unemployed youth are both a product of fragmented planning at the organisational level (or at the local community level) and of the free external labour market. Manpower planning, which is based on contractual relations between organisations, only takes care of the already employed worker but does not care for unemployed people. A welfare state type of intervention or obligatory contractual planning of manpower at levels above a given work organisation may be needed to avoid fragmentation of the external labour market.

In Czechoslovakia, finding an acceptable job is still, to a great extent, subordinated to the feasibility of getting one. Therefore, full employment and an optimal allocation of manpower is achieved while the professional and personal identification with the job on the part of the individual is relatively low. In this way, acceptability is to some extent sacrificed to feasibility, i.e. individual work alienation is exchanged for rationality of the global society.

Although the Scandinavian, combined regulation of employment seems to be comparatively preferable to the other two systems, it shares many weak points with them. It is, like the employment systems in other West and East European countries, based on a subordination of the manpower supply to the manpower demand. As in all countries throughout the world, the school system and the transition to work is guided primarily by the needs of the employment sample: the schools and the individuals as well should adapt to the demands of work organisations which create a kind of reification of the labour force. The opposite paradigm - to adapt the needs of a work organisation to the available human resources - is not established in any European country. However, we may expect that such a humanisation of employment will become more important together with the increasing strategic role of intellectual capital.

The second weak point of all the employment systems mentioned here is the limitation of employment regulations to the formal economy. When the regulation of the labour force on the labour market is surpassed by the regulation of all human resources, both feasibility and acceptability will become substantionally higher.

The fourth general shortcoming of all employment systems is due to the fact that participation of employees in looking for and creating their own jobs is still very weak. It is not only weak in East European countries but also in West European countries, and even in Yugoslavia where a system of self-management exists. Social agencies play a too paternalistic role, creating in this way too high a dependence of individual employees on their common helplessness. Individual and collective self-employment, combined with supportive systems of social agencies, might diminish these socially undesirable effects.

As a final point, all employment systems are treating education and skill in a too instrumental way. It should be stressed that education not only contributes to greater economic efficiency but also to a better quality of life and greater political democracy. Looking at education from this point of view, the redundancy of education can be seen to be a principle of civilised societies. Educational organisations should, therefore, not be limited to the needs of work organisations but should produce professional manpower in abundance. Without such a surplus, no society can create social well-being, nor will it be able to introduce structural changes and a more flexible management of social life.

Notes

1. The Labour Code guarantees the worker's right to change employment, although doing so is effected automatically only in specified instances (reasons of health, joining the husband and wife, child care, etc.). In all other instances, the Labour Code stipulates the right of the employer organisation to protect its own interests through extending the period of termination of employment by six months. The trade union organisation discusses the reasons for a worker's decision to seek other employment with each worker concerned and seeks to eliminate the causes of fluctuation. Cases in which a worker is dismissed against his/her own will are extremely rare and indeed exceptional in Czechoslovak practice and the reasons for such action are defined in detail by law.

2. The extension of compulsory school attendance to ten years - a change effected under the current reform of the education system - is motivated by this goal rather than by the interest to limit the demand for work.

3. Some parents tend to overrate the natural endowments of their own children and seek to enforce their acceptance for study at selective schools at all costs. On the other hand, there are families - by no means exceptional - who would like to see the process of vocational training shortened in the interest of a more speedy start of gainful employment.

4. The transition of secondary school leavers to university occurs in the form of an analogical system of entrance examinations. In most universities, the number of applicants for study far exceeds the number of vacancies. In the 1980s, roughly 15% of all youngsters in a single population year are enrolled for university courses of study. About a quarter of all students in day-time courses of alternative forms of study are part-time students.

7

Transition and Socialisation

Fred Mahler

The transition from school to work is one of the main socio-historical-determined processes which underlies youth in socialisation, self-assertion, and integration as an active participant in the development of adult society. Obviously, it is a complex societal reality with a contradictory nature: an arena of collisions and controversies arises between the specific goals of the school and the work system, and the dominant social structure, on the one hand, and youth's needs, aspirations, interests and value orientations, on the other. This chapter elaborates on the anticipatory-emancipatory-socialisation approach as an alternative to the other theoretical perspectives followed in studies on transition from school to work. (For a review of the functional-adaptational, the structural-generational and the life course theories, see the introductory chapter of the book.) Some of the contributions - empirical and theoretical - to this book have already implicitly followed such an approach; the attempt in this chapter, therefore, is to make this 'invisible' frame of reference 'visible' and to develop and apply this research perspective to the topic of youth unemployment. In this chapter, the theoretical roots of the anticipatory-emancipatory-socialisation approach are pointed out and then the main assumptions are briefly outlined. This conceptual framework is then used to analyse the project contributions presented in this book.

Juvenology and the Anticipatory-Emancipatory-Socialisation Approach

Youth's transition from school to work is part and parcel of the

152

whole corpus of youth research and reflects its peculiar contemporary traits. One of the main features of this research seems to be the challenge of new, holistic approaches to the traditional, fragmentary, domain-centred ('youth and work', 'youth and education', 'youth and leisure' and so on) or specialised social-science-oriented research (youth sociology, youth psychology, youth anthropology etc.).

More than ten years ago, I emphasised the need to overcome the 'crisis' in youth research through a critical approach towards traditional youth sociology as 'a monodisciplinary, predominantly descriptive approach of the younger generation, an approach which is due first of all to its functionalist orientation and to the ideological function of these researches' (Mahler, 1978). That was by no means a controversy within youth sociology as such but only directed against its errors and shortcomings, and a plea to develop the juventological approach in youth research.[1]

The search for a possible common theoretical framework for the study of the transition from school to work could get some useful insights from the already existing results based on the juventological approach (Mahler, 1983a). This framework pays great attention to the socialisation process, one of its main features being the anticipatory-emancipatory-socialisation approach.

The emphasis of traditional socialisation research on the reproductive function of the transmission and internalisation of values through education and on the resulting social status quo (Durkheim, 1977) was continued in contemporary sociology. Parsons's 'stress upon socialisation implicitly defines men as value-transmitting and value-receiving creatures rather than as value-creating creatures. Here, then, the very agency that is the source of men's humanness, socialisation, is also the agency that eternally makes a tool to pursue the ends of others; man is thus alienated in the very process of becoming human' (Gouldner, 1970). However, in the light of his analysis on 'purposive social action', Parsons accepted that socialisation also entails a prospective dimension. In developing Parsons's socialisation theory in an original way, Merton formulated the concept of anticipatory socialisation as the mechanism through which a conformity with 'non-membership groups' becomes possible.

Other Western scholars have analysed specific aspects of anticipatory socialisation.[2] These and other scholars, including many researchers from socialist countries[3], have stressed that there is a real need to radically rebuild the socialisation theory, including the one of anticipatory socialisation. Some of them argue that it is necessary to include social (class) determinism in the dynamic of the anticipatory socialisation process since those who control the present also control the future. In my view, anticipatory socialisation should be transformed from a means for social reproduction - a legitimistic and manipulatory tool for the social *status quo* - into a tool of social change and human emancipation. The juventological approach on anticipatory socialisation can be summarised as follows:

- anticipatory socialisation is an organic part of overall socialisation by means of which individuals internalise the norms and values that are socially acknowledged at present. This process takes place according to the social, economical and political power structure of the respective society and in the direction determined by objective economic and social requirements and by the dominant value system;
- anticipatory socialisation is that distinct part of the process of socialisation within which individuals develop in their value orientations and behaviours, in their needs, aspirations, plans and decisions, the possible and probable meanings of the future configuration of statuses and roles. They do this by internalising the norms and values which are socially probable in the future, or belong to the specific groups they desire to become part of. This process takes place according to the socio-economic differentiation of the statuses and roles of the groups the individuals already belong to and depend on the degree to which these persons can master their future;
- in accordance with the new orientations in education and socialisation[4] (such as: 'culture-action', Chombart de Lauwe, 1975; 'communicative competence', Habermas, 1983; 'projective education', Suchodolski, 1959; 'conscientisation', Freire, 1968; or 'anticipative and participative learning process', Botkin, Elmandjra and Malita, 1981) anticipatory socialisation has an emancipatory function. This means that it should avoid the function of *status quo* maintenance and be used instead as a tool for progressive change. This can be called the de-legitimizing role of anticipatory socialisation. It also means that anticipatory socialisation should be selective with regard to the future values, norms and requirements, taking up only those which are 'positive' and rejecting those which are 'negative' from the standpoint of human, self-

realisation goals. I call this the de-alienating role of anticipatory socialisation. It is not merely a 'selective adaptation' but more an integration through active participation in and active commitment to the change of the existing realities (Mahler, 1970 and forthcoming).

Accordingly, such a new understanding of socialisation allows it to become similar to the process of personalisation. This is the case whenever socialisation ceases to be an 'external' and 'conformist' process of moulding the personality to adapt merely to existing realities - whenever it becomes the process which offers every individual the possibility of self-assertion and self-realisation.

Such a new understanding of anticipatory emancipatory socialisation (Mahler, 1976, 1979, 1983a) makes it possible for the function of education to be changed from that of adapting young people to the already existing social opportunities and requirements, and the moulding of their aspirations in accordance with the limited possibilities, to become a factor of social change in order to fully satisfy youth aspirations.

Within this juventological, anticipatory and emancipatory socialisation approach young people in the transition process from school to work may be defined as aspiring and acting to become members of another group than their original one. Therefore, they have to learn the values of the group they want to become a member of[5] in order to be accepted, integrated and recognised by it. The change of their present value orientations and commitments in accordance with the new value orientations and commitments of the groups of which they intend to become members is, therefore, the result of an anticipatory socialisation process which proves to be essential within the transition from school to work.

Transition and Changes in the Process of Status-Role Learning and Status-Role Taking

Socialisation - mainly anticipatory and emancipatory socialisation - is directly linked to the process of role learning and role taking. The importance clearly increases in modern societies in which a change has taken place from the system of hereditary transmission of statuses (ascription) to the appropriation of roles and statuses through personal training and social action undertaken by individuals (achievement).

The transition from school to work is viewed in the light of the approach advocated here as part of the passage from the original/inherited status-role[6] through the transitory status-role towards the projected/achieved status-role. On the basis of research done by the Rumanian Youth Research Centre (Bazac *et al.*, 1974; Bazac and Mahler, 1983) the following model has been developed (see also Mahler, 1983a).

Figure 7.1: Conceptual model for changes in youth status

		present		future	
	global	present status-role		future status-role	
subjective	perceptive	perceived present status-role		projected future status-role	
	aspirational	desired present status-role		desired future status-role	
objective	actional	original status-role	transitory status-role	final status-role	
		requested present status-role		requested future status-role	
	prospective	recognised present status-role	granted present status-role	recognised future status-role	granted future status-role

(PERSPECTIVES)

While recognizing the possibility of both congruence or lack of congruence between status and role themselves, the model focuses on specific perspectives (subjective: perceptive and aspirational; objective: actional and prospective) from which the core relationship, that between the present and the future status-role can be considered. In fact, the transition process from school to work is one of the main transitory status-roles through which young people have to pass on their complex route to adulthood. This process has specific traits in every society and period; however, it is possible (and useful) to try to understand the contradictory dynamics which are connected with every specific type of transition.

The relationships between the transitory status-role and the others may be schematised as in Figure 7.2.

Figure 7.2: Relationships between status-roles

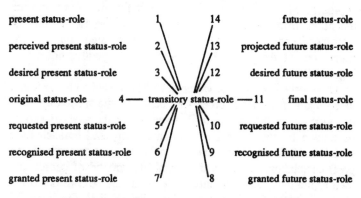

An analysis of the relationship between the transitory status-role (normally there are more than one transitory status-role which can be more or less conflicting with each other) and the other status-roles shows that a convergence or divergence can exist between them. Obviously, it is not possible to establish a general, formal, abstract rule such that only the situation when there is continuity between one or another status-role and the transitory one is 'positive'; or that the situation is 'positive' only when there is discontinuity. The model, therefore, includes contradictory functional or contradictory dysfunctional relationships as well as non-contradictory functional or dysfunctional relationships.

It also needs to be stressed that the model entails two distinctive kinds of relationships between the transitory status-role and the other status-roles: the determinative-retrospective group (nos 1-7) (ex post) and the determinative-prospective (ex ante) group (nos 8-14). The first group refers to the 'classical' socialisation process: the influence of social background (4); of existing perception (2), or aspirations (3), or value orientations (5) or of the existing social opportunities and demands (6 and 7). The second group refers to the process itself: the transitory status-role may be convergent, or not, with the final status-role (11); the desired (12), requested (10) and projected (13) status-role; and with the future, socially recognised (9) and granted (8) status-role. While the first approach is generalised in social research on youth transition from school to work, the second is present only in some of the research being done in this field. It needs to be recognised as necessary and used systematically in studies on this topic.

Much research carried out by the Youth Research Centre in Romania has had a theoretical and methodological orientation pertaining to the anticipatory and emancipatory socialisation approach. More precisely, some of the research done on the transition from school to work used a specific model of interdependencies between variables elaborated on in the framework of the juventological approach to youth studies (see Figure 7.2).

Obviously, every set of variables has to be studied in itself and in correlation with the other variables, but the most important methodological (and theoretical) issue is that the analysis should be guided by the perspective of anticipatory and emancipatory socialisation. This means that not only the past-determined (ex post) correlations (such as the social background of people and their aspirations, achievements, projects) should be considered but also the future-determined (ex ante) correlations (such as the impact of the future demands and opportunities of the labour force on professional aspirations, the influence of educational and vocational choices and projects on school and work attainment and achievements).

Actual Patterns of Transition from the Point of View of Anticipatory and Emancipatory Socialisation

The national studies undertaken in the framework of our project and other studies as well give ample documentation of the existence of a *mismatch* between the vocational aspirations of young people and their social opportunities, between the output of the educational system and the demands of the employment system at any given time. Such a mismatch is found in all European countries (and outside Europe as well). However, it takes on different forms, has different causes and, therefore, requires different solutions in the individual countries (Grootings, 1984a and 1985b).

A lot of empirical evidence could be produced in order to interpret this mismatch and its specific traits in the perspective of the anticipatory emancipatory socialisation approach. Much empirical research within the field of sociology of education, work and youth has focused on young people's vocational aspirations, projects, and careers and stressed, in a more or less comprehensive way, the contradictions between these activities and real employment opportunities. For the moment, the possibility to exhaustively synthesise all these findings is not available. Nevertheless, an attempt is made in this chapter to present some examples from this research which could allow for a confrontation between the theoretical approach and the empirical data.

From the standpoint of their research design, empirical surveys on anticipatory patterns of the transition from school to work process can be divided into three main types:

- Projective studies are the most common and extensively used. They focus on collecting information about the vocational aspirations of young people. Generally, these studies investigate educational aspirations as the means to realise specific transitions from school to work and the degree of their congruence (or lack of congruence) with the respective employment aspirations. The main interest of such studies is for the variations of these vocational aspirations resulting from structural and/or personal factors. Sometimes the motivational issue is also analysed and work-value orientations and job-prestige evaluations are requested. Youth's image of the future is depicted through the analysis of their own plans, choices and desired educational and vocational routes. The most general conclusion these studies arrive at is that the aspirations of young people are rising.

  Unfortunately, one of the main drawbacks of this research design is that it gives little insight into the relationship between the aspirations of young people and their real integration into the work force. Obviously, integration is not the result of their desires and projects only, but, rather often, the dramatic output of the mismatch between aspirations and opportunities. While such studies do document the level of subjective aspirations of young people for the future, they generally do not look into the issue of future job development - of tendencies to be found in the employment system.

  Such studies are not completely missing, however. Some authors present statistical projections on future trends in the labour market; others compare the actual structure of vocational aspirations with the structure of the professional 'objective needs' of the respective country. There are also useful cases of integrating such data in more complex research models as was done in a comparative study on youth and work undertaken in a number of socialist countries (Mitev *et al.*, 1983a). Most of these analyses have pointed out the inbalance between the rise of aspirations and the decreasing opportunities of young people to fulfil their desires. This inbalance stems from the contradiction between overqualified school leavers for available work places, resulting in an underutilisation of well-educated young people.

However useful such studies may be, the difference in the sources of the two series of data (surveys for actual aspirations and statistical forecasts for future job availabilities) creates an unavoidable bias.

- In order to overcome the shortcomings of the above-mentioned 'projective model', some researchers have used another research design which can be labelled 'retrospective studies'. Young adults who are already integrated are questioned about the successful or unsuccessful realisation of their initial vocational aspirations. Such a design is then used to establish typologies about youth employment and unemployment, based mainly on the individually and the socially determined paths of transition from school to work.

While this design has the advantage that a comparison is made by the young people themselves, it also has a weakness: the subjectivism (and resulting bias) of the reconstructed initial aspirations through a memory which can fail or misinterpret the real facts. An analysis about the future with the help of the past proves not to be very adequate either.

- So far, the best research design aimed at giving a better understanding of the impact of anticipatory socialisation on the transition process seems to be offered by longitudinal, panel, or follow-up research which includes not only an image of young people's vocational aspirations (as provided by the projective model) but also an analysis of the way in which these aspirations have (or have not) become true in the process of youth's transition from school to work. Within the scope of these studies, the subjective and objective dimensions of the genesis and the fulfilment of aspirations can both be kept under control. Moreover, this design allows for a socio-historical, concrete approach to the real paths of young people within specific social contexts, and, consequently, permits the understanding of the personal and social reasons for their desires, choices, projects, evaluations and decisions, as well as of the success or failure of their realisation.[7]

Prospective studies come to the conclusion that the mismatch between youth's aspirations, cognitive and practical skills, value orientations toward work, professional choices and vocational projects, ideals and motivations, on the one hand, and social needs and opportunities for work and the requirements of the labour market and the employment system, on the other, is the result of contradictions in the macro-structure and in the socialisation process. In turn, these contradictions have deep and negative consequences for youth's transition from school to work, for the growing up process and self-assertion of youth, for their self-realisation and their commitment to social development.

The transition process essentially refers to young people's gradual shift from a specific combination of statuses and roles - that of learning actors - to another set - that of productive actors. This shift has to be realised in specific laps of time, in particular, in micro, meso and macro contexts and under changing value orientations. Of course, this shift is determined by the concrete historical level of economic and social development and the correspondent dominant development strategy particular to the specific country in question. It has some common traits, but takes on particular shapes for individual young people dependent on their social background, on their practical chances for education and work, and on the real opportunities they have to graduate from school and enter the workforce.

The anticipatory and emancipatory socialisation approach stresses the relationship between the present (past) and the future; in this light, transition refers to the process of change experienced by young people who are channelled from a specific school system towards a specific type of work integration. Therefore, transition has to be understood as a *social space shift* from the 'world of learning' to the 'world of working' and as a *social time shift* from learning in the present to achieve future, working value orientations and behaviours.

In an ideal situation, the two 'worlds' and 'times' should not be identical but isomorphic, ensuring a harmonious, continuous and gradual passage from the one to the other, beneficial for the subjects of the process and for society as a whole. In fact, in spite of the very different shapes the process actually takes on in specific social, economic and cultural conditions, the common pattern of contemporary transition processes is a divergence between the two 'worlds' and the two 'times', which also explains the contradictory character of the transition itself.

A long-lasting and major trend in historical development, mainly within the industrial societies, has produced a time fragmentation of people's life corresponding to a social space segmentation of people's existence. The separation and opposition between the economy (the work - employment system) and education (the learning - school system) is, however, part and parcel of a larger fragmentation of social life in modern societies. This fragmentation finds its correspondent in the segmentation of human life into: childhood and youth as the learning and non-working period of life, adulthood as the working and non-learning life-period, and senior citizen as the non-learning and non-working life-period.

Furthermore, the trend in most industrial societies proves that the labour market is becoming more and more closed in regard to newcomers and that prolonged schooling, and even post-adolescence, are negative side effects of this development, which is producing large groups of permanently unemployed young people who are rejected from the employment system.

Baethge (1983 and 1985) has pointed out that the postponement of youth's integration in the workforce due to the prolongation of schooling, which, in turn, leads to a restructuring of young people's field of experience, results in work playing an increasingly smaller role in the socialisation process. As a consequence, there has been a shift from a 'productive socialisation' toward a 'consumption socialisation' at the time of adolescence. This difference of place ('productive socialisation' takes place in the work realised at home or in the firm while 'consumption socialisation' takes place at school or in other educational settings) has also led to a change in the nature of young people's social experiences and in their relationship with society and the future. Due to the technical and economic rationality predominant in industrial societies, these societies tend to avoid the socialisation of youth in and through work and to replace it through more and more abstract apprenticeship processes. The positive side of this is the freedom young people have being out of work for a longer period of time; the negative side is their isolation from and non-integration into society.[8]

More recently, fresh insights have also come from new approaches on 'segmented labour markets'. In contrast to orthodox models, segmentation theories are explicitly historical and focus on historical, systematic forces which restrict the options available to segments of the labour force. The primary unit of analysis is no longer the individual and his free choices, but rather groups or classes of individuals who face objectively different labour market situations which systematically condition their 'tastes' and restrict their range of effective choice (Carnoy, 1980). The analysis of youth aspirations and of their fulfilment or failure within the transition process from school to work is considerably enriched by the theory of the fragmentation of the labour markets. Segmentation theory alerts us to the difficulties of solving growth, distribution, and unemployment problems by simply changing the characteristics of the labour force through education and training. While education and training will certainly increase certain kinds of labour skills and may indeed contribute to growth, segmentation theory suggests that structural changes in the economy are necessary to achieve equity development and full utilisation of human resources. According to researchers like Carnoy, these structural changes imply a change in political power, for it is only with such a change that labour can win gains at the expense of capital (Carnoy, ibid.).

Against the background of such new, radical labour-market approaches, one should question whether the solution can be found in a simple matching of school and work (Levin, 1980). If the mismatch always appears to be negative because of both the impossibility to realise youth's vocational aspirations and/or inadequacy of those aspirations in relation to the real work needs and opportunities - then even the necessary good-match has to be evaluated with some restrictions. If the latter is only of a 'reproductive' character, aiming at legitimating the 'fair' educational transition towards the 'unfair', unequal positions of the income and occupational hierarchy, then such a 'correspondence' between school and work is unavoidably highly questionable. Therefore, when asking for a change of the mismatch between school and work into a good-match, the questions: What kind of good-match? In whose interests? With what aims? And by what means? also need to be asked.

Keeping in mind the real differences underlined by such concepts and models described so far, it is possible to conclude that they have a common denominator and that the general terms of the process being dealt with here can be spelled out as follows. The present transition process is characterised by the passage of young people from the ivory tower of educational and vocational aspirations and expectations and through the tunnel of the socialisation process, of educational opportunities (comprehensive or dual system) and of employment (unemployment, over-employment, underemployment) towards the labyrinth of the labour market.

The more general framework in which the transition problem has to be dealt with is the one characterised by the relationship between the 'learning world' and the 'productive world'. Against the real needs of a human-centred development aimed at overcoming the gap between school and work, it is the case that the 'autonomisation' of schooling (Adamski, 1983b) has resulted in conflict arising between these two worlds. Nevertheless, the 'responsibility' of the employment system (and the society at large) for this gap and for the resulting mismatch needs to be taken into consideration as well.

It can be assumed that the contemporary world produces a new marginalisation of young people - a prolonged youth in the ivory tower of the world of schooling, setting it more and more apart from the world of work and postponing the moment of youth's integration into social life.[9] Consequently, the 'psychosocial moratorium' (Erikson, 1970) of youth becomes the 'normal' dependent status of young people in transition. The extension of the moratorium means that there is an accentuation of youth's dependence upon adults and a prolongation of their marginal transitory status of unequal, deprived citizens - of 'second class people' because of their non-productive role of simple consumption.[10] Young people's present powerlessness and marginality is associated with their future powerlessness. In the specific conditions of their social marginalisation, youth no longer lives in time and through time but in a forced, prolonged, a temporal stage of life, devoid of present reality and without any future perspective.

Youth is always *hic et nunc*, socio-historically determined, and split into non-homogeneous groups. However, there are many indications that despite youth's obvious heterogeneous composition due to the social, cultural, ethnic and regional background of its class members, the recent changes in the status of young people increasingly serves to establish youth as a 'quasi-class' (Adamski and Staszynska in this volume). The trend towards marginalisation of larger and larger groups of youth in modern societies and the increasing lack of fulfillment of 'over-educated' young people's aspirations during the transition process proves that this is the case. While socially determined differences in the pathways and social mobility through schooling still exist, the gap between aspirations and opportunities makes young people as such (and not merely as members of one or another class or social strata) to feel more and more excluded from society.

In order to change the existing mismatch into a - let's say - good-match between youth's vocational aspirations and the demands and opportunities of the employment system, it is necessary to change the actual negative trends of the period of youth transition. This goal requires new concepts of social and economic development which could assign a participative status to young people and replace their dependence and alienation with autonomy and emancipation. To improve the transition from school to work means, therefore, not only to 'correct' its disadvantages and improve its mechanisms, but also to realise structural changes in the educational and in the work systems, and to overcome the gap between the learning and the working worlds in the context of overall social changes. This implies that we have to avoid the dichotomy of human existence in the two distinct and opposed stages: one which means learning, not working, marginality and dependence - that is, youth; and the other which means working, not learning, integration and dominance - that is, adulthood. A longterm programme of action for youth and with youth - such as that proposed within the International Youth Year - needs, therefore, a long-term effort to develop a youth science together with a theory of human development, both of which are to aim at building up social, educational and employment change programmes.

Scenarios for alternative models of transition.

The 'mismatch' discussed above proves that the actual transition process from school to work is, for the great majority of young people, to different degrees and in different forms, a critical life experience - it is a special kind of social deprivation (Adamski, Staszynska in this volume). Obviously, for some of them, it does lead to a real adjustment to the existing norms and requirements of work, to professional integration accompanied by self-realisation and satisfaction. But larger groups of each young generation are marginalised, unable to enter the workforce at all (in Western societies this is mainly due to unemployment) or forced into other professions or jobs than those desired (in Eastern countries this results primarily in performing underqualified professional activities).

From our standpoint, one of the main reasons for such a 'mismatch' is the lack of a real anticipatory and emancipatory socialisation which would provide an optimal convergence of the 'learning' and the 'productive' worlds and a flexible and open transition process between the two. The necessary change of this mismatch into a possible and desirable good-match requires a new theoretical and practical approach - to be more precise, a set of different, alternative models peculiar to the real situation in question. Instead of pretending to offer one unique, normative answer to such a complex question, some short, middle and long-term solutions that have been advocated already in different research projects and/or policy-oriented experiences are summarised here.

If the short-range future is taken into consideration, there is a rich variety of concrete targets and means for improving the transition without even challenging its actual pattern:

- Many, if not all, contributors to this debate emphasise, first of all, necessary changes in the school system itself. Linking school closer with work implies changes in the functions and contents of education, in school organisation, curricula, recruitment of pupils and assignment of graduates (Gelpi, 1979, UNESCO, 1980). The actual or proposed patterns for changes in the school system aiming at a better transition from school to work range from the structures which maintain the separation in time and space of school and work while trying to realise a maximal isomorphism of education and labour, on the one hand, and the integration of school and work, on the other hand.
- In order to avoid, or reduce, unemployment as well as all other kinds of mismatches between youth's aspirations and training, on the one hand, and social (economic) opportunities and needs, on the other, educationalists and social planning experts are suggesting new forms of transition from school to work which include larger possibilities of choice and adaptation for school leavers and better means for the employment system to select and integrate the new labour resources in the economic system.

- Last but not least, short-run reforms concern the improvement of the employment system itself, while every society faces far more difficult problems as a result of the complexity and rigidity of the already established systems; whenever it has to adapt to new requirements, there are numerous new experiences and proposals with regard to changes which could prove to be useful for a better transition of young people from school to work. In this context, one can point to the new trends in work organisation, which are connected not only with technological change but also with the need to enrich and humanise productive work (Grootings *et al.* 1988), or the self-management experiences, or the new co-operative trends in the work organised by young people, mainly the unemployed themselves (Hartmann, 1985).

Some analyses and programmes try to integrate all three of these components of the transition process into more general reforms as, for example, the ideas about the recurrent school system viewed in the light of lifelong education (Faure *et al.* 1972; Husen, 1974; Schwartz, 1981). Although only some examples of possible, desirable and sometimes already existing changes in the transition process have been presented here - and these are quite necessary and useful - such changes cannot solve the problem itself because it requires structural solutions.

Such intended structural changes will unavoidably clash with the already existing structures of the school and employment systems and with the conservative and inertial reactions of those with vested interests in keeping the *status quo*. Consequently, they cannot be discussed without referring to the main macro-social and political issues of every society.

Long-term goals could be realised through a step by step process of improvements in the transition from school to work: reforms of school and work are to be undertaken for the realisation of these aims; but in order to know which are our actual choices, we have to better know where we are going and where it would be desirable to go tomorrow and the day after.

A counter-model of the present conflicting system of education and work - a unique alternative transition model - cannot be established for all countries in an abstract and normative way. Moreover, the need to consider not a one-dimensional but rather a multidimensional set of alternative models of change for the existing transition pattern is grounded in the necessity to leave the future open for every new generation, to avoid 'the colonisation of the future' and to allow each generation its freedom of choice and invention. Nevertheless, it could be useful to submit a theoretical approach of a possible set of scenarios or different models to be further discussed, tested and improved while continuing to take into account the need to adapt them to every particular situation.[11] The anticipatory and emancipatory socialisation approach is, if not the best, at least one of the possible theoretical frameworks for such an endeavour.

In the light of this approach, the essential, common trait of the different alternative models of transition could be schematised as shown in Figure 7.3.

Figure 7.3: Two types of socialisation

Socialisation type A: from learning to working

PAST	PRESENT	FUTURE
inherited	transitory	achieved
status-role	learning status-role	working status-role

Socialisation type B: from learning and working to working and learning

inherited	transitory	achieved
status-role	learning and working status-role	working and learning status-role
FAMILY SETTING	EDUCATIONAL SETTING	OCCUPATIONAL SETTING

Socialisation type A (present socialisation), even while training young people for life and for integration in social and economic development by ensuring a strong isomorphism between their present educational statuses and roles and their future occupational statuses and roles, preserves the separation of these in time and space. With socialisation, type B transition becomes radically different; it requires an essential transformation of educational statuses and roles in order to bring together, in various forms and degrees, the elements that are constitutive of the learning and working statuses and roles. Furthermore, it requires correspondent changes in the occupational statuses which, in the light of lifelong education, have to be not only working - but also learning statuses and roles. The transition process is fundamentally changed within model B because education and work are no more separated in time and space since man's life is no more divided into a learning and non-working stage and a working and non-learning stage.

We could visualise this shift as presented in Figure 7.4.

Figure 7.4: Fragmented and integrated types of socialisation

Present   Fragmentation

Future   Integration

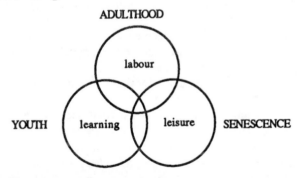

Obviously, such a change requires a more general shift in society at large in line with a new understanding and strategy of human development and its economic educational and social patterns.

Nevertheless, transitional and achieved statuses and roles will not lose their distinctiveness. The transitory status-role of learning and production, while having a new feature, will still continue to have a predominant learning orientation; similarly, the new occupational status-role, while becoming suitable for exercising both working and learning functions, will continue to have a predominant working feature. Such a possible and necessary change requires transformations in the content, goals and forms of the socialisation process, accentuating its anticipatory and emancipatory character. This means, *inter alia*, that it should avoid any mechanical submittal of school and education to the pragmatic, technocratic demands of the existing productive system, such as, for instance, in the case of the transposition of the factory model into schools. In fact, even in the conditions of the new transition model, the school milieu cannot and must not be identified with the productive one, but only become transformed in order to become, as much as possible, convergent with the employment milieu.

Changes in the transition process demand, therefore, apart from transformation of the school- and work systems, a shift in the general social context from 'maldevelopment' towards 'good-development' and, at the international level, a new economic and educational order (Gelpi, 1984, Mahler, 1983b and forthcoming).

***

The transition process reminds us of the multisecular practice of youth 'rites of passage' through which young people were 'initiated' in order to become adults. As van Gennep (1960) described, these ceremonials which celebrated the individual's or group's passage from one status to another, were in most cases built up of three stages: separation of the individuals (or the group) from their previous condition; transition or limen (in French: *marge*) when the individuals (or the group) are in a state of suspension, in limbo; and incorporation (in French: *aggregation*) or integration into their new status. While continuing the ancient 'rites of passage', modern societies have up to now lengthened youth as a marginalised status in the prolonged adolescence limbo.

The high interest of so many contemporary scholars in this problem is significant and encouraging at the same time. Here are two more arguments. King states that the 'first technological/educational idiom' of pre-industrial times and the actual 'second technological/educational idiom' specific for the industrial society are superseded by the 'third technological/educational idiom' which is called upon by the newly emerging, post-industrial society and the new information technologies. This new idiom is 'marked by the divergence in the development of new skills in a far wider range of people and jobs, with alternation of working and learning and life-experiences, with lifelong reappraisal and feedback to incorporate the experiential dimension of education and re-education' (King, 1986). As a conclusion to his historical analysis of the impact of the social division of labour upon the social division of education, Visalberghi stresses the possibility to overcome the cultural mutation that has separated and opposed manual and intellectual work in hierarchical, class societies by splitting education and work, through a 'counter-mutation' which could create new societies - classless and horizontal - aiming at integrating learning and working, education and labour in modern ways (1979).

Some of the readers of this chapter - as well as some of the colleagues involved in this project - will possibly evaluate the underlying outlook of this approach as merely utopian. Yet, some utopian order to really change (hopefully for the better) the existing, almost ungratifying, social realities defended by a positivistic legitimate social science is needed. It is also necessary to give more room to the social creativity of individuals and groups, and to the commitments of young generations to structural transformations. Therefore, the option social scientists have is and remains to strive for a realistic utopianism which could mix the freedom of imagination with a concrete approach towards individual and collective real needs and their possible fulfillment.

Which are the new perspectives which the future already opens for the change in the period of youth's transition from school to work? Could this transition be transformed from an alienating mismatch into a self-realizing and emancipatory good-match, and, if so, how? This latter question is one which not only has to be analysed but also answered with the participation of youth itself.

Notes

1. Most recently by Pearl, 1985. The UNESCO World Conference on Youth, organised during the International Youth Year, also stressed that in order to overcome the theoretical ambiguity of the concept of youth, it is necessary to integrate youth research into a broader theoretical framework and mentioned the suggestions of many specialists to define such research as 'the social science of youth', (UNESCO, 1985a).

2. Authors like Adamski, 1983b; Mitev, 1982; and Rosenmayr, 1983, have used the concept with different meanings. See, amongst others: Boudon, 1973; Bourdieu, 1974; Bourdieu and Passeron, 1970; Bowles and Gintis, 1976; Herriot, 1984; Kreutz, 1974; Rosenmayr, 1969 and 1983.

3. See especially Friedrich and Müller, 1980; Meier, 1974; Shubkin, 1968; Mitev, 1982.

4. These new orientations are manifest in concepts such as 'culture-action' developed by Chombart de Lauwe, 1975; 'communicative competence' by Habermas, 1983; 'projective education' by Suchodolski, 1959 and 1960; 'conscientisation' by Freire, 1968; the 'anticipative and participative learning process' by Botkin *et al.*, 1981.

5. Merton carefully stresses that while anticipatory socialisation is functional in relatively open social structures, it becomes dysfunctional in relatively closed social structures where the individual 'would not find acceptance by the group to which he aspires and would probably loose acceptance, because of his outgroup orientation, by the group to which he/she belongs. This latter type of case will be recognised as that of the marginal man, poised on the edge of several groups but fully accepted by none of them' (Merton, 1968) In fact, the young person who is not able to fulfil his/her own aspirations during the process of transition from school to work becomes the victim of aspirations he/she cannot achieve and of hopes he/she cannot satisfy just like the 'marginal man'.

6. Under status-role we understand, in a reformulation of the functionalist concepts, the integrated position and function of the social actor within the social process (see Mahler, 1983a, p. 195).

7. Studies that have come close to the prospective design can be found in Flanagan and Cooley, 1966; Bachman, 1970; Friedrich and Müller, 1980; Mitev *et al.*, 1983a; ISFOL, 1984; and Hartmann and Stefanov, 1984. A number of contributions to our research project have also followed a prospective design.

8. This and other recent analyses of the specific features of youth's experiences within the worlds of 'education' and 'production' remind us of Bourdieu's research on schooling habits and *causalité du probable* (Bourdieu and Passeron, 1970; Bourdieu, 1974); Bernstein's contributions to the study of educational codes (Bernstein, 1975); Bowles's and Gintis's studies on contradictory socially determined schooling life paths and their divergent ways of integration in the labour market (Bowles and Gintis, 1976); Margaret Archer's studies on macro-structural determinism of educational systems (Archer, 1979) and the studies about youth subcultures, including the shift towards 'post-materialism' (Inglehart, 1977) and so on.

9. While referring to the situation of adolescence becoming, in modern times, more than just a passage from childhood to adulthood - specifically, a 'new category in the spectrum of life phases' - Leopold Rosenmayr stresses the 'sociostructural determination of life phases' and inquires into the peculiar consequences of the new social, economic and value changes upon the status change of youth. 'The "favored adolescence" of secondary schools (has) emerged as a period free of work obligations, in this respect similar to the retirement phase. Here one can see very clearly how life phases are connected with the division of labour and with institutional or legislative changes...' (Rosenmayr, 1983). Other

authors have used different concepts for the same phenomenon: 'post-adolescence' is used by Kenniston 1968; 'extended-youth' by Adamski, 1985b; and 'prolonged' or 'forced youth' by Rus and Drobnic, 1984.

10. Henrick Kreutz - who stressed the importance of a specific loss in status (*Statusverlust*) for young people - has also pointed out the complex interplay, within the time perspective and its changes (*Wandel der Zeitperspektive*), between the projected and the realised statuses - as the main reason for the insecurity youth feels during the transition with regard to the full adult status which is refused to them as young people (Kreutz, 1974).

11. This claim can also be found in Angela Little's overview of main shifts in the conceptual emphasis on educating/learning and employing/working interrelationships; this author asks for an 'interactive model of education and work simultaneously assimilating each other and acting on each other - or of supply and demand supplying and demanding of each other...' (Little, 1986).

List of References

Adamski, W. (1968) 'The life orientations of the younger and older generations of Poles', *International Journal of Political Education*, no. 3, pp. 255-69

Adamski, W. (1983a) 'Education and careers in today's Poland: aspirations and opportunities', European Institute of Educational and Social Policy, occasional paper no. 10, Amsterdam

Adamski, W. (1983b) 'Youth research and theories. Recent trends in cross-systems and cross-cultural perspectives', paper submitted to the United Nations' University, Tokyo, Japan

Adamski, W. (1983c) 'The young generation as an agent of social change'. In: P. Mitev *et al.* (eds) *Sociology of Youth: Mexico 1982. Collection of materials presented at the sessions of RC34 'Sociology of Youth' at the X World Congress of Sociology*, vol. 2, Sofia, pp. 125-40

Adamski, W. (1984) 'Cross-cultural differences in educational and occupational aspirations of young employees: Poland and Czechoslovakia'. In: P. Grootings (ed.), *Youth and work in Europe*, vol. II, Vienna Centre-Moscow, Moscow, pp. 79-85

Adamski, W. (1985a) 'On systemic determinants and possible dimensions in comparing aspirations, values and work orientations of East and West European youth in transition from school to work', working document for the Vienna Centre International Workshop, Castelgandolfo, April

Adamski, W. (1985b) 'Some conceptual remarks on the topic: youth transition from school to work'. In: P. Grootings and M. Stefanov (eds), *Transition from school to work*, Sofia, pp. 29-34

Alaluf, M., Desmarez, P. and Domb, I. (1983) 'Life patterns of poorly educated young unemployed people in the Charleroi region'. In: *Growing up without work*, European Centre for Work and Society, Van Gorkum, Assen

AMS-Statistics (1985) *Sammanfattningen av ungdomsstatistiken fr februari* (Summary of youth statistics for February), Stockholm, 11 March

Andersen, N.B. *et al.* (eds) (1979) *The impact of systems change in organisations. Results and conclusions from a multinational study of information systems development in banks*, Sijthoff and Noordhoff, Alphen aan den Rijn

Andics, J. (1983) 'Youth studies and social practice in Hungary'. In: P.E. Mitev *et al.* (eds) *Sociology of Youth: Mexico 1982. Collection of materials presented at the sessions of RC34 'Sociology of Youth' at the X World Congress of Sociology*, vol. 1, Sofia, pp. 19-34

Archer, M. (1979) *Social origins of educational systems*, Sage, London

Babushkina, T. and Shubkin, V. (1984) 'On the Problem of Transition from School to Work', working document for the International Workshop on New Technologies, Youth Employment and Transition from School to Work, Sofia, November

References

Babushkina, T. (1985) 'Some problems of the transition of young people from school to work in the Soviet Union'. In: P. Grootings and M. Stefanov (eds), *Transition from school to work*, Sofia, pp. 367-78

Bachman, J.G. (1970) *Youth in transition*, I.S.R., Michigan

Baethge, M., Gerlach, F. and Müller, J. (1980) 'Zu den Veränderungen des Übergangs Jugendlicher von der Schule in Arbeit und Beruf in den siebziger Jahren', *WSI Mitteilungen II*, pp. 660-7

Baethge, M., Schomburg, H. and Voskamp, U. (1983) *Jugend und Krise - Krise aktueller Jugendforschung*, Campus, Frankfurt/Main/New York

Baethge, M. (1984) 'The significance of work for young people under the current situation in the Federal Republic of Germany'. In: P. Grootings (ed.) *Youth and work in Europe*, vol. II, Vienna Centre-Moscow, Moscow, pp. 29-40

Baethge, M. (1985) 'L'individualisation comme espoir et danger: apories et paradoxes de l'adolescence dans les sociétés occidentales', *Revue Internationale des Sciences Sociales, La Jeunesse*, no. 106, pp. 479-91

Battistoni, L. (1984) 'New Technologies, Youth Employment and Transition from School to Work', working document for the International Workshop on New Technologies, Youth Employment and Transition from School to Work, Sofia, November

Bazac, D., Dumitrescu, I., Mahler, F. and Radulian, V. (1974) *Geneza si dinamice idealului in adolescenta*, Scrisul romanesc, Craiova

Bazac, D. and Mahler, F., (1983) *Profesia mea*, CCPT, Bucharest

Bazac, D., *et al.* (1986) *Tineret, munca, integrare*, Editura politica, Bucharest

Benz-Overhage, K., Brumlop, E., von Freyberg, Th. and Papadimitriou, Z. (1982) *Neue Technologien und Alternative Arbeitsgestaltung. Auswirkungen des Computereinsatzes in der Industriellen Produktion*, Campus Verlag, Frankfurt/Main/New York

Bernstein, B. (1975) *Towards a theory of educational transmissions, class, codes and control*, Routledge and Kegan Paul, London/Boston

Bialecki, I. (ed.), *Zmiany ruchliwosci spolecznej* (Changes in Social Mobility), in print

Botkin, J.W., Elmandjra, M. and Malita, M. (1981) *Orizontul fara limite al invatarii* (No limits to learning), Editura politica, Bucharest

Boudon, R. (1973) *Education, opportunity and social inequality*, John Wiley Press, New York

Boudon, R. (1973a) *L'inégalité des chances*, Armand Colin, Paris

Bourdieu, P. and Passeron, J.C. (1970) *La Reproduction*, Les Editions de Minuit, Paris

Bourdieu, P. (1974) 'Avenir de classe et causalité du probable', *Revue francaise de sociologie*, vol. XV, janvier-mars

Bowles, S. and Gintis, H. (1976) *Schooling in capitalist America*, Basic Books, New York

Brandt, G., Kundig, B., Papadimitriou, Z. and Thomae, J. (1978) *Computer und Arbeitsprozeß. Eine Arbeitssoziologische Untersuchung der Auswirkungen des Computereinsatzes in Ausgewählten Betriebs-abteilungen der Stahlindustrie und des Bankgewerbes*, Campus Verlag, Frankfurt/Main/New York

Braverman, H. (1974) *Labor and Monopoly Capital: The Degradation of Work in the Twentieth Century*, Monthly Review Press, London

Brossard, M. and Maurice, M. (1974) 'Existe-ti-il un Modèle Universel des Structures d'Organisations?', *Sociologie du Travail*, no. 4, pp. 403-26

Burawoy, M. (1985) *The Politics of Production. Factory Regimes under Capitalism and Socialism*, Verso, London

Butera, F. and Thurman, J.E. (1984) *Automation and Work Design. A Study prepared by the International Labour Office*, North Holland, Amsterdam, New York, Oxford

Carnoy, M. (1980) *Segmented labour markets, in education, work and employment*, International Institute for Educational Planning, Paris

Casal, J., Ludevid, M., Medio, M. and Planas, J. (1984) 'The Transition from School to Work in Spain', working document for the International Workshop on New Technologies, Youth Employment and Transition from School to Work, Sofia, November

CEDEFOP (1981) *Youth unemployment and alternance training in the EEC*, CEDEFOP, Berlin

CERI (1983) *Education and Work. The views of the young*, OECD, Paris

Charvát, F. and Sak, P. (1984) *Faktory sociálního a ekonomického rozvoje mládeze* (The factors of social and economic development of working youth), Institute for Philosophy and Sociology, Czechoslovak Academy of Sciences, Prague

Cherednicenko, G. and Shubkin, V. (1985) *Molodezh vstupaet v zhizn* (Youth enter life), Misl, Moscow

Child, J. (1986) 'Technology and Work: An outline of Theory and Research in the Western Social Sciences'. In: P. Grootings (ed.) *Technology and Work. East-West Comparison*, Croom Helm, London, pp.7-65

Chombart de Lauwe, P.H. (1975) *La Culture et le Pouvoir*, Ed Stock, Paris

Clarke, O. (1985) 'The work ethic. An international perspective', paper, Paris

CMEA (1983) *Statistical Yearbook*

Coleman, J.S. (1961) *The adolescent society*, Glencoe Free Press, New York

Coleman, J.S. (1974) *Youth: Transition to Adulthood*, U.S. Government Printing Office, Washington D.C.

Comte, C. (1983) *New patterns of behaviour and attitudes of young people regarding work in industralised countries: a partially annotated bibliography*, IILS, Geneva

Cooper, C. and Mumford, E. (eds) (1979) *The quality of working life in Western and Eastern Europe*, Associated Business Press, London

References

Crouch, C. and Pizzorno, A. (1978) *The resurgence of class conflict in Western Europe since 1968*, 2 volumes, Macmillan, London

De Santis, G. and Ventrella, A.M. (1984) 'The relationship between young people and work in Italy'. In: P. Grootings (ed.), *Youth and Work in Europe*, vol. I, Vienna Centre-Moscow, Moscow, pp. 58-87

Diederen, J. (1981) 'From year to year: the passage of young people from different social backgrounds through primary and secondary education in the Netherlands', *The Netherlands' Journal of Sociology*, pp. 1-21

Diederen, J. (1983a) *De keuze van een beroep. Van jaar tot jaar* (Occupational choice), ITS, Nijmegen

Diederen, J. (1983b) *Van Jaar tot Jaar, derde fase: de keuze van een beroep* (From year to year, third phase: the choice of an occupation), ITS, Nijmegen

Dinkova, M. (1984) 'Problems of social policy towards working parents'. In: P. Grootings (ed.), *Youth and work in Europe*, vol. II, Vienna Centre-Moscow, Moscow, pp. 115-22

Dore, R. (1973) *British Factory - Japanese Factory. The Origins of National Diversity in Industrial Relations*, University of California Press, Berkeley/Los Angeles

Drobnic, S. (1984a) 'Strukturne spremembe v brezposelnosti' (Structural changes of unemployment). In: Antoncic, Drobnic, Rus, and Svetlik (eds) *Tokovi zaposlovanja*, Moderna organizacija, Kranj

Drobnic, S. (1984b) 'Transition from School to Work in Yugoslavia', working document for the International Workshop on New Technologies, Youth Employment and Transition from School to Work, Sofia, November

Dubois, P. and Makó, C. (1980) La Division du Travail dans l'Industrie. Etudes de Cas Hongrois et Francais, *Groupe Sociologie du Travail*, Paris

Düll, K. (1975) *Industriesoziologie in Frankreich. Eine historische Analyse zu den Themen Technik, Industriearbeit, Arbeiterklasse*, Europäische Verlagsanstalt, Frankfurt/Main

Durkheim, E. (1977) *Education et sociologie*, PUF, Paris

Edwards, R. (1979) *The Contested Terrain*, Heineman, London

Elder, G. H. (1981) 'History and the life course'. In: D. Berteaux (ed.), *Life History Approach in the Social Sciences*, Sage Publications, Beverly Hills

Emeljanov, Y.V. (1986), *Obostrenie sozialno-politicheskih protivorechii v SShA y molodezh*, Moscow, pp. 54-5.

Erdész, T. and Molnár, P. (1986) *A fiatalok iskolázottsága pályakeztdésük idején* (Utilisation of education at the professional start), Mankuatigyi Szemle, Budapest

Erikson, E.H. (1970) *Jugend und Krise*, Ferdinand Enke Verlag, Stuttgart

Eyraud, F. *et al.* (1984) 'Dévelopements des qualifications et apprentisage par l'entreprise des nouvelles technologies: le cas des machines-outils à commande numérique (MOCN) dans l'industrie mécanique', *Sociologie du Travail*, vol. XXVI, no. 4, pp. 482-99

Eyraud, F. and Rychener, F. (1986) 'A Societal Analysis of New Technologies'. In: P. Grootings (ed.) *New Technology and Work. East-West Comparison*, Croom Helm, London, pp. 209-30

Faure, E., *et al.* (1972) *Apprendretre*, UNESCO, Paris

Fend, H. (1981) *Theorie der Schule*, P.T., Munich-Vienna-Baltimore

Ferge, Zs. and Häler, J. (1974) *Az iskola szociológiai probléma*, Budapest

Flanagan, J.C. and Cooley, W.W. (1966) *Project talent: one year follow-up studies*, University of Pittsburgh/Project Talent, Pittsburgh

Forslin, J., Sarapata, A. and Whitehill, A.M. (1979) *Automation and Industrial Workers. A Fifteen Nation Study*, vol. 1, part 1, Pergamon Press, Oxford

Forslin, J., Sarapata, A. and Whitehill, A.M. (1981) *Automation and Industrial Workers. A Fifteen Nation Study*, vol. 1, part 2, Pergamon Press, Oxford

Fragnière, G. and Doorten, K. (1984) 'Proposals for a youth policy'. In: P. Grootings (ed.) *Youth and Work in Europe*, vol. II, Vienna Centre-Moscow, Moscow, pp. 132-9

Freire, P. (1968) *The pedagogy of the oppressed*, Herder and Herder, New York

Friedman, A. (1977) *Industry and Labour*, Macmillan, London

Friedrich, W. and Müller, H. (1980) *Zur Psychologie der 12 bis 22 jährigen*, Berlin

Galland, O. and Louis, M.V. (1984) 'Attitudes of young French unemployed youth towards work'. In: P. Grootings (ed.) *Youth and Work in Europe*, vol. II, Vienna Centre-Moscow, Moscow, pp. 148-58

Galland, O. (1985) 'Formes et transformations de l'entrée dans la vie adulte', *Sociologie du Travail*, vol. XXVII, no. 1, pp. 32-52

Gallie, D. (1978) *In Search of the New Working Class: Automation and Social Integration within the Capitalist Enterprise*, Cambridge University Press, London

Gazsó, F. and Shubkin V. (eds), (1980) *Trudyashayasya molodezh: orientazii y zhiznenie pouty. Opyt sravnitelnogo sociologicheskogo issledovania* (Working youth: orientation and life path. Experiment of comparative sociological study), Budapest

Gazsó, F., Laki, L. and Molnár, P. (1984) *Pályakezdök az iparban* (Professional Start in Industry), MSZMP KB Társadalomtudományi Intézete, Budapest

Gelpi, E. (1979) 'A future for lifelong education', *Work and education*, Manchester monographs 13, vol. 2

Gelpi, E. (1984) 'Introduction: education et nouvel ordre mondial', *Education et Société*, no. 6, avril-mai

Gennep, A. van (1960) *The rites of passage*, The University of Chicago Press, Chicago

Gorz, A. (ed.) (1976) *The division of labour*, Harvester Press, Brighton

Gouldner, A.W. (1970) *The coming crisis of western sociology*, Basic Books, New York

References

Greve, R.M. and Gladstone, A. (1984) 'Analysis of changes and differences in the attitude and behaviour of young people concerning work'. In: P. Grootings (ed.), *Youth and Work in Europe*, vol. II, Vienna Centre-Moscow, Moscow, pp. 74-5.

Grootings, P. (ed.) (1984a) *Youth and Work in Europe*, vol. I + II, Vienna Centre-Moscow, Moscow

Grootings, P. (1984b) 'Youth and work in comparative perspective'. In P. Grootings (ed.) *Youth and work in Europe*, vol. II, Vienna Centre-Moscow, Moscow, pp. 183-98

Grootings, P. and Stefanov, M. (eds) (1985a) *Transition from School to Work*, Institute of Youth Studies, Sofia

Grootings, P. (1985b) 'Transition from school to work: towards an international comparative analysis'. In P. Grootings and M. Stefanov (eds) *Transition from school to work*, Sofia

Grootings, P. (ed.) (1986a) *Technology and Work. East-West Comparison*, Croom Helm, London

Grootings, P. (1986b) 'Technology and Work: A Topic for East-West Comparison?' In P. Grootings (ed.) *Technology and Work. East-West Comparison*, Croom Helm, London, pp. 275-301

Grootings, P., Gustavsen, B. and Héthy, L. (eds) (1988) *New forms of work organization in Europe*, Transaction Publishers, New Brunswick

Gustavsen, B. (1984) 'Automation and Work Organisation: Policies and Practices in Market Economy Countries'. In: *International Labour Office*, pp. 75-114

Habermas, J. (1983) *Cunoastere si comunicare*, Editure politica, Bucharest

Haller, M. and Mach, B.W. (1984) 'Structural changes and mobility in a capitalist and a socialist society; comparison of men in Austria and Poland'. In: M. Niessen, J. Peschar and Ch. Kourilsky (eds), *International Comparative Research. Social Structures and Public Institutions in Eastern and Western Europe*, Pergamon Press, Oxford, pp. 43-103

Hartmann, J. (1977) 'Samhllsfrndring och ungdomsa rbetlshet' (Societal change and youth unemployment). In I. Hellberg (ed.), *Ungdomens problem p arbetsmarknaden* (The problems of youth on the labour market), University of Göteborg, Göteborg

Hartmann, J. (1984) *Youth in the welfare society*, Uppsala

Hartmann, J., and Stefanov, M. (1984) *Youth in Europe: integration through participation*, Sofia-Vienna

Hartmann, J. (1985) *Transition from School to Work in Sweden*, unpublished paper

Hartmann, J. (1986) *To live on the brink. Causes and consequences of the decrease in youth unemployment in Europe*, forthcoming

Heinemann, K. (1978) *Arbeitslose Jugendliche. Ursachen und individuelle Bewältigung eines sozialen Problems. Eine empirische Untersuchung*, Luchterhand, Darmstadt/Neuwied

Herriot, P. (1984) *Down from the ivory tower. Graduates and their jobs*, John Wiley Press, New York

Hirschorn, L. (1984) *Beyond mechanization. Work and technology in a post-industrial age*, MIT Cambridge, Mass.

Hoffman, A. (1984), 'Aspects of the Transition from School to Work in the German Democratic Republic', working document for the International Workshop on New Technologies, Youth Employment and Transition from School to Work, Sofia, November

Hoffman, A. (1985) 'The Transition from School to Work', working document for the Vienna Centre International Workshop, Barcelona, September

Holsinger, D.B. (1978) 'The national longitudinal study: policy implications to youth'. Paper presented at the Polish-American Symposium on Social Structure and Educational Policy, Chicago, October, 1978

Hoss, D. (1986) 'Technology and Work in the two Germanies'. In: P. Grootings (ed.) *Technology and Work. East-West Comparison*, Croom Helm, London

Hövels, B. (1984) 'Recent Dutch Studies on the Transition from School to Work', working document for the International Workshop on New Technologies, Youth Employment and Transition from School to Work, Sofia, November

Hövels, B. and Vissers, A. (1984) 'Changing attitudes and behaviour of young people towards work: the Dutch situation'. In: P. Grootings (ed.), *Youth and Work in Europe*, vol. I, Moscow-Vienna Centre, Moscow, pp. 34-56

Hübner-Funk, S. (1983) 'Life perspectives of West-German Youth after 40 years of European Peace', paper presented at expert meeting of the European Centre for Social Welfare Training and Research, Talberg, Sweden

Hungarian Statistical Yearbook (1974)

Husen, T. (1974) *The learning society*, Methuen, London

IILS (1978) 'Social aspects of work organization: implications for social policy and labour relations' Selected papers and proceedings of an international symposium, Geneva

IILS (1983) 'Changing perceptions of work in industrialized countries: their effect on and implications for industrial relations', papers of an international symposium, Geneva

ILO (1979) *New forms of work organization*, vol. I + II, Geneva

ILO (1984) *Year Book of Labour Statistics*, Geneva

Inglehart, R. (1977) *The silent revolution changing values and political styles among Western publics*, Princeton University Press, Princeton, N.J.

International Labour Conference (1986) *Report V: Youth*, ILO, Geneva

ISF München (ed.) (1976) *Betrieb, Arbeitsmarkt, Qualifikation*, EVA, Frankfurt/Main/Munich

ISFOL (1984) *Tapporto ISFOL sulla formazione professionale*, Franco-Angelli, Milan

Kavcic, B. (1986) 'Self-management and Technology'. In: P. Grootings (ed.) *Technology and Work. East-West Comparison*, Croom Helm, London, pp. 103-38

Kenniston, K. (1968) *Young radicals*, Harcourt, Brace and World, New York

References

Kenniston, K. (ed.) (1971) *Youth and Dissent*, Harcourt, Brace and World, New York

Kern, H. and Schumann, M. (1984) *Das Ende der Arbeitsteilung? Rationalisierung in der industriellen production: Bestandsaufnahme, Trendsbestimmung*, Verlag C. H. Beck, Munich

Kerr, C. *et al.* (1973) *Industrialism and industrial man*, Penguin Books, Harmondsworth

King, E.J. (1986) 'Responses to a new technological/occupational structure required of the educational system' *Ricerca educativa*, anno II, no. 1

Kiuranov, T. (1985) 'L'attitudes des jeunes à l'égard du travail: le cas de la Bulgarie', *Revue Internationale des Sciences Sociales*, no. 106

Kluckhohn, C. (1951) 'Values and value orientations in the theory of action'. In: T. Parsons and E.A. Shils (eds) *Toward a general theory of action*, Harvard University Press, Cambridge, Mass., p. 389

Knapp, I. (1984a) 'The behaviour of Austrian youth on entering employment'. In: P. Grootings (ed.), *Youth and work in Europe*, vol. I, Vienna Centre-Moscow, Moscow, pp. 123-47

Knapp, I. (1984b) 'New Technologies, Youth Employment and Transition from School to Work', working document for the International Workshop on New Technologies, Youth Employment and Transition from School to Work, Sofia, November

Köditz, V. (1981) *Sozialer und materieller Status von Jugendlichen beim Übergang von der Schule zum Beruf*, Synthesebericht, CEDEFOP, Berlin

Koistinen and Urponen (eds) (1984) *New Technologies and Social Development*, Joensuu

Korosic, M. (1985) 'Neki problemi usmjeravanja raspodjele dohotka' (Problems of regulation of income allocation), paper presented at the Workshop on Contradictions of the Public Ownership, Skopje

Kreutz, H. (1974) *Soziologie der Jugend. Grundfragen der Soziologie*, Hrsg. Dieter Unessens, Band 9, Juventa Verlag, Munich

Kreutz, H. and Wuggenig, U. (1978) 'Auswirkungen der Jugendarbeitslosigkeit - Versuch einer Diagnose', *Deutsche Jugend*, 26 Jg., pp. 491-502

Kudera, S. (1977) 'Organisations-strukturen und Gesellschafts-strukturen. Thesen zu einer Gesellschaftsbezogenen Reorientierung der Organisations-soziologie', *Soziale Welt*, no. 28, pp. 16-38

Kulpinska, J. (1986) 'The Concept of Technology in the Sociology of Socialist Countries'. In P. Grootings (ed.) *Technology and Work. East-West Comparison*, Croom Helm, London, pp. 67-101

Lammers, C.J. and Hickson, D.J. (eds) (1979) *Organizations Alike and Unlike. International and Institutional Studies in the Sociology of Organizations*, Routledge and Kegan Paul, London

Lammers, C.J. (1983) *Organisaties vergelijkenderwijs*, Het Spectrum, Utrecht

Laumann, E.O. (ed.) *Social Stratification*, Bobbs-Merrill, Indianapolis-New York

Levin, Henry M. (1980) *Workplace democracy and educational planning in education, work and employment*, International Institute for Educational Planning, Paris

Little, A. (1986) 'From educating and employing to learning and working' *Prospects*, vol. XVI, no. 1

Lojkine, J. (1982) 'Crise et Renouveau de la Sociologie du Travail (A propos du Paradigme Techniciste)', *Sociologie du Travail*, no. 2, pp. 192-206

Louis, M.V. (1984) 'Attitudes of young French unemployed youth towards work'. In: P. Grootings (ed.), *Youth and work in Europe*, vol. I, Vienna Centre-Moscow, Moscow, pp. 151-3

Ludevid, M. (1984) 'Young People and Work in Spain'. In: P. Grootings (ed.), *Youth and Work in Europe*, vol. II, Vienna Centre-Moscow, Moscow, pp. 88-101.

Lutz, B. (1976) 'Bildungssystem und Beschäftigungsstrukturen in Deutschland und Frankreich. Zum Einfluß des Bildungssystems auf die Gestaltung Betrieblicher Arbeitskräftestrukturen'. In: ISF München (ed.), *Betrieb, Arbeitsmarkt, Qualifikation*, Frankfurt/Main/Munich

Lutz, B. (1984) 'Technik und Arbeit: Stand, Perspektiven und Probleme Industriesoziologische Technikforschung'. In: Koistinen and Urponen (eds) *New Technologies and Social Development*, Joensuu, pp. 59-87

Magnussen, B. (1981) 'What is being done in Sweden for unemployed 16- and 17-year-olds?', *Current Sweden*, no. 275

Mahler, F. (1970) 'Youth and development: from marginality to engagement', unpublished paper presented at the Varna World Congress of Sociology

Mahler, F. (1976) *Dimension axiologique dans la sociology des aspirations*. In: Chombart de Lauwe (ed.) *Transformations de l'environement, des aspirations et des valeurs*, Ed du CNRS, Paris

Mahler, F. (1978) 'From youth sociology to juventology', unpublished paper presented at Uppsala World Congress of Sociology

Mahler, F. (1979) 'Aspirations et creativité sociale', *Revue de l'Institut de Sociologie*, no. 3-4

Mahler, F. (1981) 'Integrating education with production and research in Romania', *Prospects*, vol. IX, no. 4

Mahler, F. (1983a) *Introducere in juventologie*, Editure stintifica si enciclopedica, Bucharest

Mahler, F. (1983b) 'Juventology and Youth Social Development'. In: P. Mitev *et al.* (eds) *Sociology of Youth: Mexico 1982. Collection of materials presented at the sessions of RC34 'Sociology of Youth' at the X World Congress of Sociology*, vol. I, pp. 43-56

Mahler, F., (1985) 'Transition from School to Work in Romania'. In: P. Grootings and M. Stefanov (eds), *Transition from School to Work*, Sofia, pp. 289-327

Mahler, F. (forthcoming) *Development alternatives: from maldevelopment towards gooddevelopment, from marginality towards participation*

References

Makó, C. (1986) 'Organisational innovation and the social conditions of the labour process', paper, Institute of Sociology, Budapest

Marcuse, H. (1964) *One-dimensional man: studies in the ideology of advanced industrial society*

Marglin, S.A. (1976) 'What do bosses do? The origins and functions of hierarchy in capitalist production'. In A. Gorz (ed.), *The divisions of labour*, Harvester Press, Brighton, pp. 13-54

Marsden, D. and Duff, E. (1975) *Workless. Some unemployed men and their families*, Penguin Books, Harmondsworth

Maurice, M. (1980) 'Le Determinisme Technologique dans la Sociologie du Travail (1955-1980). Un changement de paradigme?', *Sociologie du Travail*, no. 1, pp. 22-37

Maurice, M., Sorge, A. and Warner, M. (1980) 'Societal Differences in Organizing Manufacturing Units: A Comparison of France, West Germany and Great Britain', *Organization Studies*, no. 1, pp. 59-86

Maurice, M., Sellier, F. and Silvestre, J.J. (1982) *Politique d'Education et Organisation Industrielle en France et en Allemagne*, PUF, Paris

Maurice, M. *et al.* (1986) *Des Enterprises en Mutation dans la Crise. Apprentisage des Technologies Flexibles et Emergence de Nouveaux Acteurs*, LEST, Aix en Provence

Mead, M. (1970) *Culture and commitment. A study of the generation gap*, The Museum of Natural Science History, New York

Meier, A. (1974) *Soziologie des Bildungswesens*, Volk und Wissen, Berlin

Merton, R.K. (1968) *Social theory and social structure*, The Free Press, New York

Mitev, P. (1980) 'Social Activeness of Youth', *Bulgarian Journal of Sociology*, vol. 3, Institute of Youth Studies, Sofia

Mitev, P.E. (1982) *Sociology facing the problems of youth*, Institute of Youth Studies, Sofia

Mitev, P.E. (1983a) *La sociologie face aux problèmes de la jeunesse*, Institute of Youth Studies, Sofia

Mitev, P.E. (1983b) 'Youth aspirations and social strategies'. In: P. Mitev *et al.* (eds) *Sociology of Youth: Mexico 1982. Collection of materials presented at the sessions of RC34 'Sociology of Youth' at the X World Congress of Sociology*, vol. 2, Institute of Youth Studies, Sofia, pp. 115-24

Mitev, P.E., Shubkin, V., Gospodinov, K. and Gazsó, F. (1983a) (eds) *Youth and Labour*, Institute of Youth Studies, Sofia

Mitev, P.E. (eds) (1983b) *Sociology of Youth: Mexico 1982. Collection of materials presented at the sessions of RC34 'Sociology of Youth' at the X World Congress of Sociology*, vol. 1 + 2, Institute of Youth Studies, Sofia

Mitev, P.E. (1984) 'Changes in the attitudes of Bulgarian youth towards work'. In: P. Grootings (ed.) *Youth and work in Europe*, vol. 1, Vienna Centre-Moscow, Moscow, pp. 197-217

Molnar, P. (1984a) 'The Hungarian youth's attachment to a vocation as shown by an international comparison'. In: P. Grootings (ed.), *Youth and work in Europe*, vol. II, Vienna Centre-Moscow, Moscow, pp. 93-104

Molnar, P. (1984b), 'School Career and the First Job', working document for the International Workshop on New Technologies, Youth Employment and Transition from School to Work, Sofia, November

Morgan, D.H.J. (1975) *Social Theory and the Family*, London

Mrela, K. and Kostecki, M.J. (1981) 'Incompatible Studies on Comparable Organizations: Looking for Way-Out from a Dead-End Street in Organizational Research': In: K. Mrela and M.J. Kostecki, *Barriers and Perspectives. Studies in the sociology of organizations*, Polish Academy of Sciences, Institute of Philosophy and Sociology, Warsaw

Neuner, G., (1985) *Pädagogik*, no. 9, p. 658.

Noble, D. (1979) 'Social Choice in Machine Design: the Case of Automatically Controlled Machine Tools'. In: A. Zimbalist, *Case Studies on the Labor Process*, Monthly Review Press, New York, pp. 18-50

Noelle-Neumann, E. (1978) *Werden wir alle Proletarier? - Wertwandel in der Gesellschaft*, Interfrom, Zürich

OECD (1980) *Youth unemployment, the causes and consequences*, Paris

OECD (1984) *The nature of youth unemployment. An analysis for policy-makers*, Paris

Parsons, T. and Shils E.A. (eds) (1951) *Toward a general theory of action*, Harvard University Press, Cambridge, Mass.

Parsons, T. (1964) *Social structure and personality*, The Free Press, London

Pearl, A. (1985) 'Tendances théoriques de la recherche sur la jeunesse aux USA', *Revue International des Sciences Sociales, La Jeunesse*, no. 106, p. 500

Richta, R. (1969) *Civilization at the Crossroads. Social and Human Implications of the Scientific and Technological Revolution*, International Arts and Sciences Press Inc., Prague

Roberts, K. (1985) 'La jeunesse des années 80: un nouveau mode de vie', *Revue Internationale des Sciences Sociales*, no. 106

Rose, M. (1979) 'Servants of the Post-Industrial Power', *Sociologie du Travail in Modern France*, MacMillan, London

Rosenbrock, H. R. (1983) 'Engineers and the work that people do', paper, University of Manchester, Institute of Science and Technology, Manchester

Rosenmayr, L. (1969) *Jugend*, Ferdinand Enke Verlag, Stuttgart

Rosenmayr, L. (1972) 'Introduction: nouvelles orientations théoriques de la sociologie de la jeunesse', *Revue Internationale des Sciences Sociales*, vol. XXIV, no. 2, pp. 227-71

Rosenmayr, L. (1976) *Jugend. Handbuch der Empirischen Sozialforschung*, Band 6, Hrsg. von René König, Ferdinand Enke Verlag, Stuttgart

Rosenmayr, L. (1983) 'Biography and identity in aging and life course transitions: an interdisciplinary perspective'. In: T.K. Hareven and K.J. Adams (eds), The Guilford Press, New York/London

Rothwell, R. and Zegveld, W. (1979) *Technical change and employment*, Frances Pinter, London

References

Rus, V. (1985a) 'Interorganizational Analysis of Competence', paper prepared for the International Workshop ISA: Competence, Trade Unions and Self-Management, Osnabrück

Rus, V. (1985b) 'Kriza izobrazevanja in zaposlovanja' (The crisis of education and of employment). In: Jerovsek, Rus and Zupanov (eds) *Kriza jugoslovenskog drustva*, Globus, Zagreb

Rus, V. and Drobnic, S. (1985) 'The role of the employment system in transition from school to work', working document for the Vienna Centre International Workshop, Castelgandolfo, April

Sawinski, Z. and Domanski, H. (1986) *Wymiary struktury spolecznej. Analiza porównawcza* (Dimensions of social structure, A Comparative Analysis), Ossolineum, Warsaw

Schaff, A. (1985) *Wohin führt der Weg?* Europa Verlag, Vienna

Schwartz, B. (1981) *L'insertion professionnelle et sociale des jeunes*, La documentation française, Paris

Shaiken, H. (1984) *Work transformed. Automation and labor in the computer age*, Holt, Reinhard and Winston, New York

Shubkin, V.N. (1968) 'Choix professional des jeunes', *Revue Francaise de Sociologie*, vol. IX, no.1, janvier-mars

Shubkin, V. (1970) *Soziologicheskie opyty* (Sociological experiments), Moscow

Shubkin, V. (1979) *Nachalo pouty: Problemy molodezhi v zerkale soziologii y literatury* (Beginning of the path: the problems of youth in the mirror of sociology and works of fiction), Moscow

Shubkin, V. (1984) 'On a possible trend of all European research projects on the social problems of young people'. In: P. Grootings (ed.) *Youth and Work in Europe*, vol. II, Vienna Centre-Moscow, Moscow, pp. 173-82

Skolverstyrelsen (1985) *Kommunernas uppfljningansvar fr ungdomar under 18r* (Follow-up responsibility of municipalities for youth under 18), Stockholm

Sorge, A. (1980) *Cultured Organization*, IIM paper 80-9, International Institute of Management, Berlin

Sorge, A., Hartmann, G., Warner, M. and Nicholas, I. (1981) *Microelectronics and Manpower in Manufacturing: Applications of Computer Numerical Control in Great Britain and West Germany*, IIM/LMP 81-16, Wissenschaftszentrum Berlin

Starr, J.M. (1981) 'Adolescence and resistance to schooling: a dialectic', *Youth and Society*, vol. 13, no. 2

Stefanov, M. (1983) *The student: life plans and self-realization* (in Bulgarian), Sofia

Stefanov, M. (1984), 'The Transition from School to Work (An Attempt at a Sociological Approach to the Problem)', working document for the International Workshop on New Technologies, Youth Employment and Transition from School to Work, Sofia, November

Stegmann, H. (1984) 'Analysis of changes and differences in the attitudes and behaviour of young people towards work'. In: P. Grootings (ed.), *Youth and Work in Europe*, vol. II, Vienna Centre-Moscow, Moscow, pp. 86-92

Suchodolski, B. (1959) *Trattato di pedagogia generale*

Suchodolski, B. (1960) *Pedagogia dell'essenza e pedagogia dell'esistenza*

Suvar, S. (1977) *Skola i tvornica* (The school and the factory), Pedagoska biblioteka, Zagreb

Svetlik, I. (1984) 'Ali imamo trg delovne sile?' (Do we have a labour market?). In: Antoncic, S. Drobnic, V. Rus and I. Svetlik (eds) *Tokovi zaposlovanja*, Moderna organizacija, Kranj

Tanko, Z. (1985) 'Teoretsko opredeljivanje drustvene svojine' (The theoretical definition of public ownership), paper presented at the Workshop on Contradictions of Public Ownership, Skopje

Taylor, M. (1983) 'Growing up without work: a study of young unemployed people in the West Midlands'. In: *Growing up without work*, European Centre for Work and Society, Assen, Van Gorkum

Thompson, P. (1983) *The nature of work. An introduction to debates on the labour process*, Macmillan, London

Treiman, D.J. (1970) 'Industrialization and social stratification'. In: E.O. Laumann (ed.), *Social Stratification*, Bobbs-Merrill, Indianapolis-New York, pp. 207-34

Tyree, A., Semyonov, M. and Hodge, R.W. (1979) 'Gaps and glissandos: inequalities, and social mobility in 24 countries', *American Sociological Review*, no. 44, pp. 410-22

UNESCO (1979) *Youth and Work. The incidence of the economic situation on the access of young people to education, culture and work*, Paris

UNESCO (1980) International meeting of experts on the promotion of work in education, ED-80/CONF 627/7

UNESCO (1981) *Youth in the 1980s*, Paris

UNESCO (1985a) *From Grenoble to Barcelona: progress to date and future prospects*, proceedings of the World Congress on Youth, Barcelona, 8-15 July, SHS-85/CONF 401/7

UNESCO (1985b) *Papers presented at the meeting of experts on youth unemployment*, Paris, September

Venedikov, J. *Problems of the self-realization of those completing secondary education*, (a report from a study kept at the information bank of the Institute of Youth Studies) (in Bulgarian), Institute of Youth Studies, Sofia, pp. 19-22

Visalberghi, A. (1979) 'Education et division du travail en Occident, Apprendre et travailler, Le point de Perspectives', Z. Morsy (ed.) UNESCO, Paris

Viteckova, J. and Hudecek, J. (1984) 'Youth and work in Czechoslovakia'. In: P. Grootings (ed.), *Youth and work in Europe*, vol. I, Vienna Centre-Moscow, Moscow, pp. 161-96

Volanen, M.V. (1984a) 'Young people and working life in Finland'. In: P. Grootings (ed.), *Youth and work in Europe*, vol. I, Vienna Centre-Moscow, Moscow, pp. 102-22

Volanen, M.V. (1984b) 'How Does a Young Adult Settle Down in a Vocation?', working document for the Vienna Centre international workshop, Lauf

Wacker, A. (1978) *Vom Schock zum Fatalismus? Soziale und psychische Auswirkungen der Arbeitslosigkeit*, Campus Verlag, Frankfurt/Main/New York

References

Wilkinson, B. (1983) *The Shopfloor Politics of New Technology*, Heinemann, London

Wilpert, B. (1984) 'Youth and work in the Federal Republic of Germany - recent research evidence'. In: P. Grootings (ed.), *Youth and work in Europe*, vol. I, Vienna Centre-Moscow, Moscow, pp. 23-33

Worotynska, K. (1984) 'Transition from school to work. Poland 1973-1984', working document for the International Workshop on New Technologies, Youth Employment and Transition from School to Work, Sofia, November

Zavalloni, M. 'Values'. In: H.C. Triandis and R.W. Brislin (eds) *Handbook of cross-cultural psychology, social psychology*, Allyn and Bacon Inc., vol. 5, p. 75

Zey-Ferrel, M. and Aiken, M. (1981) *Complex organizations: critical perspectives,* Scott, Foresman and Company, Glenview Illinois

Zimbalist, A. (1979) *Case Studies on the Labor Process*, Monthly Review Press, New York

Appendix
Questionnaire for national reports

1. What are the chances of young people in the age group of 15-
    25 (after leaving compulsory education) for

    - further general education
    - vocational training
        * apprenticeship
        * school
    - work
    - unemployment

Please give figures from 1974-1983, for different types of
schooling, sex and age groups.

2. What is the typical process of transition from school to work
    for the different types of school leavers, sex and age groups?

    What are the dominant patterns for school leavers to find a
    job?

    Did any serious changes occur during the last 10 years in both
    typical processes and dominant patterns?

3. Who is the major actor in finding the first job?

    - the family
    - the labour office
    - the enterprise
    - others

Please give the empirical details.

4. Please give an overview of the discussions (with empirical
    data) on the influence of the following developments on the
    transition from school to work

- demographic developments
- changes in the educational system
- changes in qualification levels
- changes in the employment system
- technological changes

5. What is the degree of mobility of young people during the first five years of their occupational career (voluntary or forced)?

6. Which jobs/professions in your country are considered to be more/less attractive?

   What are the relevant dimensions of a job (salary, content, etc.) that enter these evaluations?

7. How does the employment system (enterprises, etc.) react to the increased number of school leavers and/or the higher qualifications of the young labour force in terms of

   - selection mechanisms
   - changed organisation and division of work
   - segmentation of labour force
   - classification and salary systems
   - others

8. What is known from sociological studies about tensions and conflicts between younger and older generations on the labour market and in the work organisation?

9. How do young people cope with (or react to) problems in the transition from school to work?

   - with continuation of education
   - with withdrawal from the formal employment system and/or entry in the informal system
   - with intensified competition
   - etc.

Please specify for specific subgroups.

10. What is the reaction of the educational system and the state?

The Authors

Wladyslaw Adamski (1930), Professor of Sociology at the Institute of Philosophy and Sociology, Polish Academy of Sciences, Warsaw, Poland.

Lea Battistoni (1944), Researcher at the Institute for the Development of Vocational Training (ISFOL), Rome, Italy.

Jo Diederen (1940), Researcher at the Institute for Applied Social Sciences (ITS) of the University of Nijmegen, Nijmegen, The Netherlands.

Sonja Drobnic (1956), Assistant Researcher at the Institute of Social Research, Ljubljana, Yugoslavia.

Juri Emeljanov (1937), Researcher at the Institute of the International Labour Movement of the Soviet Academy of Sciences, Moscow, Soviet Union.

RoseMarie Greve (1947), Research Associate at the International Institute of Labour Studies, Geneva, Switzerland.

Peter Grootings (1951), From 1981 until 1987 Research Coordinator at the European Coordination Centre for Research and Documentation in Social Sciences (Vienna Centre), Vienna, Austria. Since 1987 Project Director at European Centre for the Development of Vocational Training (CEDEFOP), Berlin (West).

Jürgen Hartmann (1944), Professor of Sociology at the University of Uppsala, Sweden.

Achim Hoffmann (1946), Head of the Department of Youth and Education, Institute of Youth Research, Leipzig, German Democratic Republic.

Ilan Knapp (1944), Director of the Österreichisches Institut für Berufsbildungsforschung (ÖIBF), Vienna, Austria.

The authors

Marie-Victoire Louis (1943), Researcher at the Groupe d'étude sur la division sociale et sexuelle du travail, Paris, France.

Fred Mahler (1930), Senior Researcher at the Youth Research Centre, Bucarest, Romania.

Peter Molnar (1942), Researcher at the Institute of Social Studies, Budapest, Hungary.

Jordi Planas (1951), Professor of Sociology of Education at the Autonomous University of Barcelona, Spain.

Veljko Rus (1929), Professor of Sociology and Researcher at the Institute of Social Research, Ljubljana, Yugoslavia.

Gustavo de Santis (1939), Professor of Sociology of Work at the University of Rome and Researcher at the Institute for Studies on Economic and Technological Development (ISVET), Rome, Italy.

Vladimir Schubkin (1923), Professor of Sociology at the Institute of the International Labour Movement of the Soviet Academy of Sciences, Moscow, Soviet Union.

Katarzyna Staszynska (1954), Research Assistant at the Institute of Philosophy and Sociology of the Polish Academy of Sciences, Warsaw, Poland.

Michael Stefanov (1942), Deputy Director and Researcher at the Institute of Youth Studies, Sofia, Bulgaria.

Anna-Maria Ventrella (1943), Director of the Institute for Studies on Economic and Technological Development (ISVET), Rome, Italy.